Legal Transcription in Canada

REVISED EDITION

Lynn M. Berry and Barbara L. Asselin

emond ▪ Toronto, Canada ▪ 2013

Emond Montgomery Publications Limited
60 Shaftesbury Avenue
Toronto ON M4T 1A3
http://www.emond.ca/highered

Printed in Canada.
Reprinted February 2019.

We acknowledge the financial support of the Government of Canada. **Canadä**

Acquisitions and development editor: Bernard Sandler
Supervising editor: Paula Pike
Copy editor: Deanna Dority
Production editor: Jim Lyons
Proofreader: Diane Gula
Cover designer: Tara Wells
Cover image: kutaytanir/iStockphoto

Library and Archives Canada Cataloguing in Publication

Berry, Lynn M., author
    Legal transcription in Canada / Lynn M. Berry and Barbara L. Asselin. — Revised edition.

Includes index.
ISBN 978-1-55239-585-1 (pbk.)

    1. Legal transcription—Canada—Handbooks, manuals, etc.   2. Legal assistants—Canada—Handbooks, manuals, etc.   I. Asselin, Barbara L., author   II. Title.

KE355.L4B47 2013   652.3'26   C2013-903299-1

To Les, Nathan, Myles, and Blake,
and in memory of my loving mother, Fredda Moore,
who could always pull me through

—Love, Lynn

To Mike, Casey, and Jamie

—Love, Barb

Contents

CHAPTER 3 Wills and Powers of Attorney

CHAPTER 4 Estates

CHAPTER 5 Real Estate

CHAPTER 6 Corporations

CHAPTER 7 Family Law

CHAPTER 8 Civil Litigation

CHAPTER 9 Criminal Law

CHAPTER 10 Intellectual Property

CHAPTER 11   Landlord and Tenant

CHAPTER 12 Small Claims

Preface

Welcome to *Legal Transcription in Canada*!

Legal transcription is a skill that is used in law offices. Lawyers rely on their assistants to transcribe correspondence, legal documents, notes, memos, voice messages, and tasks.

In order to be proficient at transcription, there are other skills that need to be honed as well. These are a general understanding of the areas of practice and the associated terminology, correct usage of grammar and punctuation, and keying citations.

This textbook is intended for anyone who wishes to strengthen these skills, and there are 11 areas of practice covered.

Detailed instructions have been provided for transcribing using a computerized software program and for keying citations.

We hope you enjoy working for Berry & Asselin LLP!

CHAPTER 1

Introduction

I. OVERVIEW OF TEXTBOOK

This student textbook is divided by chapter into areas of legal practice and provides exercises to build strength in transcription while honing your citation and grammar skills. In order to understand the transcriptions, a brief introduction and terminology exercise is built into each chapter for general knowledge. All chapters contain the following structure:

A. Introduction

Each chapter's introduction provides general overviews of the 11 areas of practice contained in this textbook.

B. Terminology Exercises

Exercises are based on the introduction of each area of practice and the vocabulary found in the voice files.

C. Citation Exercises

Exercises are based on statutes, regulations, and case law for federal, provincial, and territorial legal citations.

D. Grammar Rules

Each unit focuses on a different area of grammar or punctuation.

E. Grammar Exercises

Exercises are based on the grammar or punctuation rule that is the focus of the chapter.

F. Beginner Voice Files

Voice files consist of letters, memos, and voice messages with basic vocabulary.

G. Intermediate Voice Files

Voice files consist of letters, memos, and voice messages with more advanced vocabulary and word-processing techniques, and are longer in length.

H. Advanced Voice Files

Voice files consist of letters, memos, voice messages, legal documents, statements of account, and legal citations.

II. OVERVIEW OF LEGAL TRANSCRIPTION

Transcription is one of the most common ways that lawyers communicate with their assistants. Lawyers dictate letters, memos, instructions to their assistants, and changes or paragraphs in legal documents. The lawyers can dictate at any time and in any location using hand-held devices. They dictate in their offices, cars, homes, airports, courthouses, or wherever it is convenient. For this reason, the quality of the dictation will vary due to background noises.

It takes some time to learn the dictators' accents and practices in terms of punctuation, acronyms, and abbreviations. Some lawyers will provide the paragraph breaks, spelling, and punctuation, while others will leave it for you to do. Lawyers will dictate material and then tell you to delete it because they have changed their minds. They will also make changes at the end of the dictation because they have thought of something else they wanted to say. You will have to insert these changes into the keyed text. No dictation will be perfect from start to finish!

Transcription is a skill. It takes time to develop in order to work effectively. Transcription will strengthen your listening, grammar, proofreading, punctuation, and vocabulary skills.

Transcription voice files are created by lawyers using various devices such as voice recorders, or the voice recording function on an MP3 player, iPod, or other personal device. The voice files are then downloaded from the device to the assistant's computer using a USB connection.

Transcribing these downloaded voice files can be done using desk transcribers or computer software. You will be using a computer software program to transcribe voice files in this textbook.

When transcribing, listen to a phrase or meaningful group of words and key it. When you become more experienced at transcription, you will be listening to the next group of words while you are keying the previous one. Listen to the dictator's voice to guide you for pauses, which will assist you in correct punctuation. If you don't understand a word, listen to it again. Listen to the words before and after it for context. Avoid introducing errors by using words that change the meaning of the dictation - do not key text that does not make sense! Once you have finished the transcription, you should listen to the voice file again and compare it with your keyed document for accuracy.

You have to use your resources, these being a dictionary, client files, a thesaurus, Internet sites for postal codes and addresses, specialized reference books, and your own common sense.

III. COMPANY OVERVIEW

The company we will be using throughout this textbook will be Berry & Asselin LLP. It is a full-service law firm that practises in the following areas of law:

A. Wills and Powers of Attorney

B. Estates

C. Real Estate

D. Corporations

E. Family Law

F. Civil Litigation

G. Criminal Law

H. Intellectual Property

 I. Landlord and Tenant

J. Small Claims

When the transcriptions in this textbook refer to correspondence, memos, statements of account, voice messages, or documentation from lawyers or staff of our firm, you will use an address of one of our satellite offices based upon where you are located. Your professor may also create a customized address for the firm. The choices are:

A. Eastern Satellite Office:

    Berry & Asselin LLP
    1 Justice Circle
    Halifax, NS   B3J 1H8

B. Central Satellite Office:

    Berry & Asselin LLP
    1 Justice Circle
    Toronto, ON   M3J 1H8

C. Western Satellite Office:

    Berry & Asselin LLP
    1 Justice Circle
    Vancouver, BC   V3J 1H8

D. Customized Satellite Office:

    Alternatively, you can replace the city and province with your resident city and province. Using the customized option, please change the first letter of the postal code to the one used in your municipality.

Our law firm comprises lawyers (both partners and associates), paralegals, law clerks, legal assistants, and other administrative staff. Please refer to the organizational chart at Figure 1.1 for the hierarchy of the legal personnel of the firm.

Figure 1.1   Hierarchy of Legal Personnel of Berry & Asselin LLP

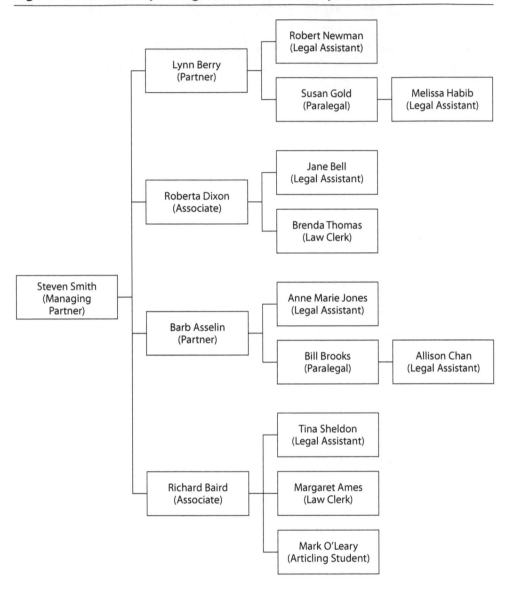

Please refer to Figure 1.2 for a complete list of the administrative staff of the firm.

Figure 1.2   Administrative Personnel of Berry & Asselin LLP

You work at Berry & Asselin LLP as a **floater**. A floater is an administrative assistant who works on a variety of files for a variety of lawyers, instead of working for only one lawyer. A floater usually fills in for other administrative staff when they are sick or on holidays. Floaters also do overflow work when other administrative staff members are very busy and have more work than can be done by one person.

IV. TEMPLATES

Files have been created for your use as follows:

A. Letterhead

B. Interoffice memorandum

C. Voice message

D. Statement of account

E. Will

F. Undertaking

V. TRANSCRIPTION INSTRUCTIONS

You will need the following equipment in order to install and use the transcription software referred to in this textbook:

A. Computer

B. Internet connection

C. Headphones

The software we will be using for the transcriptions in this textbook is called **Express Scribe**. Follow these steps to install the software:

A. Plug your headphones into the headphone jack on your computer or your computer's speakers.

B. Open your Internet browser and navigate to the following website:

www.nch.com.au/scribe/index.html

If this URL does not work, simply open your Internet browser, go to www. google.com and enter the words "express scribe" or "express scribe free transcription software" into the search box. Then click on the resulting link to the new www.nch.com website.

C. Click the "Get it now" button.

D. Click "Run" on the following pop-up screen (Figure 1.3).

Figure 1.3   Dialogue Box Upon Download of Express Scribe Software

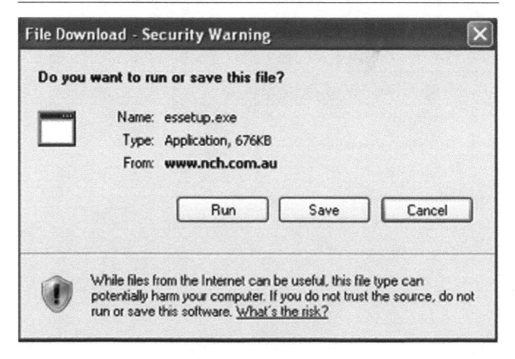

E. Click "Run" again on the following pop-up screen (Figure 1.4).

Figure 1.4   Confirmation to Run Express Scribe Software

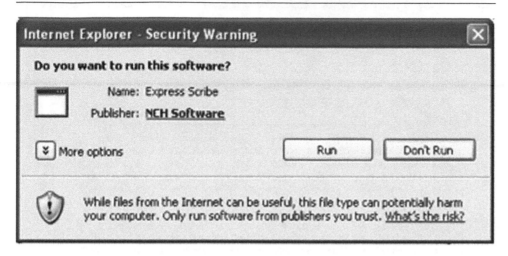

F. Click "Run" a third time on the following pop-up screen (Figure 1.5).

Figure 1.5   Confirmation to Run Set-up File for Express Scribe Software

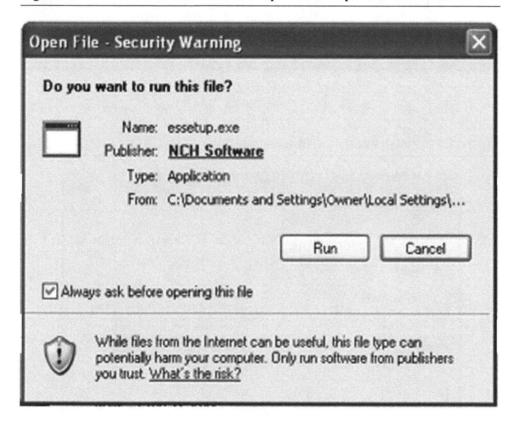

G. The next screen (Figure 1.6) will be the Express Scribe License Agreement. Click "I agree with these terms" and then click "Next."

Figure 1.6   Confirmation of Agreement With Terms of License Agreement

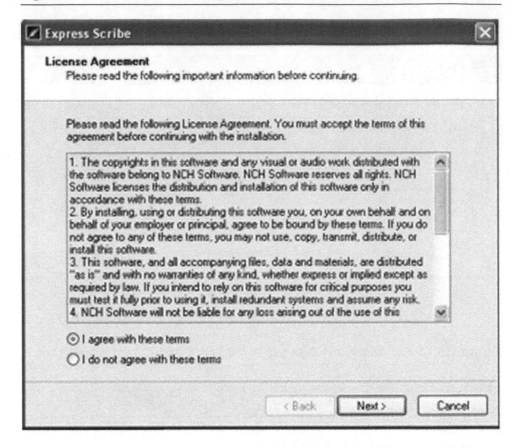

H. The program will install. Click "Finish" on the final pop-up screen (Figure 1.7).

Figure 1.7   Finish Express Scribe Installation

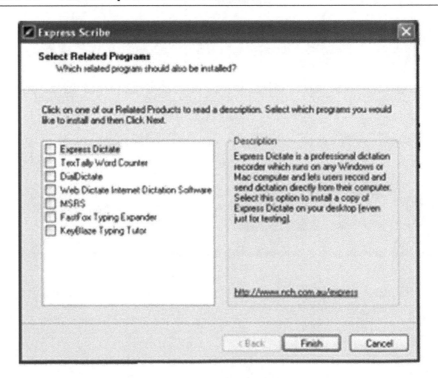

I. The program will launch automatically, along with a recording of how to use the program (Figure 1.8).

Figure 1.8   Initial View of Express Scribe Software

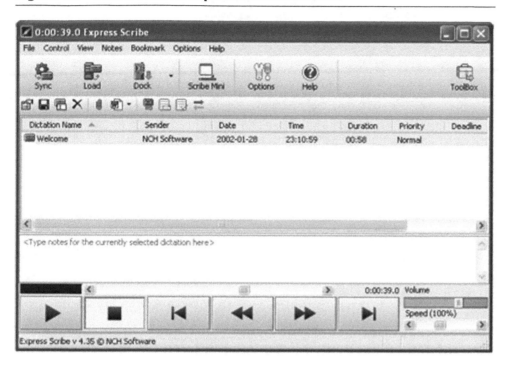

J. You can use the following **hot keys** to control the program:

1. F9 Play

2. F4 Stop

3. F7 Rewind

4. F8 Fast Forward

5. Ctrl + Home = Go to the beginning of the transcription

6. Ctrl + End = Go to the end of the transcription

Now that you have installed the required software, you need to create a folder on your computer's C:\ drive, or a drive specified by your professor, and call it "Transcription." Save all your transcription files in this directory.

To load voice files into the transcription software, click on the "Load" button. Navigate to the newly created Transcription folder on your computer. Click "OK," and you will see any voice files that are in your folder (Figure 1.9).

Figure 1.9   How to Save Voice Files for Use in Express Scribe

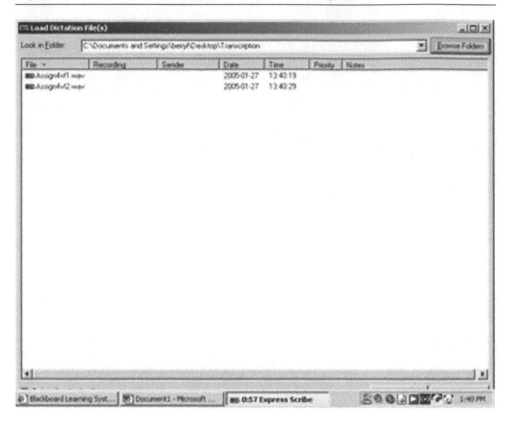

Click on a voice file to begin listening. Use the above keyboard shortcuts or hot keys to stop and start as necessary. You may have your word-processing software open for keying and minimize the Express Scribe software. You can still use the keyboard shortcuts while the program is minimized.

VI. LEGAL CITATIONS

Legal citations are written references to published or unpublished sources, and there are specific rules that must be followed when presenting a citation. The most common method of citing in Canada is the McGill Guide (*Canadian Guide to Uniform Legal Citation*, 6th ed. [Toronto: Carswell, 2006]). There are also resources on the Internet that demonstrate this method.

Lawyers require citations to be listed in trial briefs, factums, memorandums of law, trial records, and other legal correspondence and documents.

An example of a citation is:

Thomson v Thomson, [1994] 3 SCR 551.

It is your responsibility, as the legal assistant, to be able to accurately present the citations.

A. Textbook Citations

Each chapter has three primary sources of citations: statutes, regulations, and case law. Citations are from federal, provincial, and territorial jurisdictions.

B. Chapter Citation Exercises

Each chapter has two exercises in writing citations. The first exercise has citations as units in a mixed order and you must rewrite each citation in the proper order. The second exercise has the citations in the correct order; however, each citation has spacing, formatting, or punctuation errors, and you must rewrite the citations accurately.

C. Resources for Verifying Citations

If you are unfamiliar with citation rules, it is good practice to look up the citations for verification once you have keyed them. The best references to use are Quicklaw and Westlaw Canada; however, you may not have access to the software, as there is a charge for using it unless you have an education account.

The two most popular free sites for verifying citations are:

1. Supreme Court of Canada decisions found at

   http://scc-csc.lexum.com.

   Use the advanced search feature and search by case name or key words (Figures 1.10–1.12).

Figure 1.10   Supreme Court of Canada Website

Figure 1.11   Supreme Court Judgments Advanced Search Page

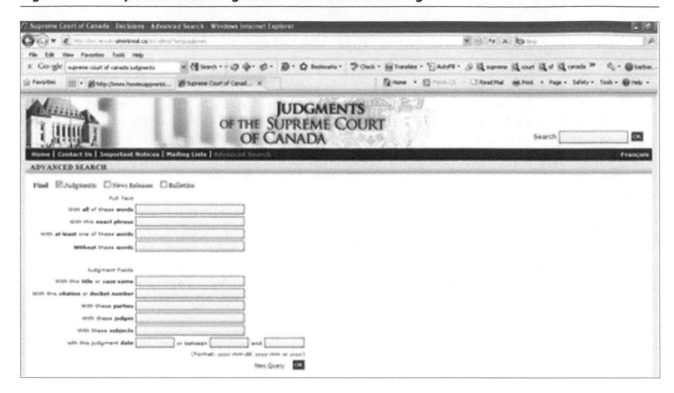

Figure 1.12   Advanced Search Results Page

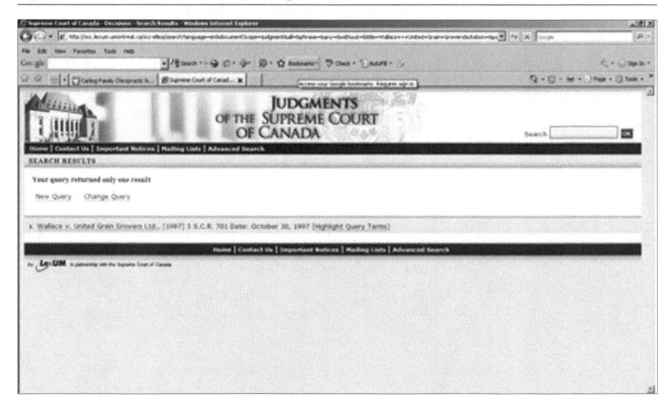

2. CanLII found at

www.canlii.org.

There are databases for federal decisions as well as for each province and territory. You can search by inserting the citation, statute name, regulation name, or case name under full text or under statute name/case name. You can also insert the decision date to narrow the search (Figure 1.13).

Figure 1.13   CanLII Search All Databases Page

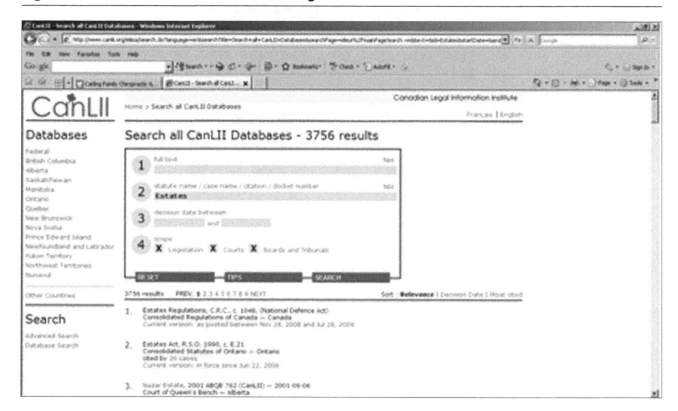

You must keep in mind that citation rules must be applied; however, the above sites are a good start for cross-referencing. Neutral citations should appear first when citing; however, on the sites, you may see them written last. You must correct this in your citing. An example of a neutral citation is 2007 ABQB 60. Neutral citations are explained in greater detail under F. Case Law.

D. Statutes

Statutes are laws that have been passed by the legislative bodies at the federal, provincial, and territorial levels. They are referred to as acts.

Every year, Canada and each province and territory publish volumes containing all new acts passed during the previous legislative year, as well as amendments to existing acts. These volumes of statutes (S) are identified by the year, such as Statutes of Canada 1989 (SC 1989) and Statutes of Ontario 1991 (SO 1991).

At stated intervals, every ten years in Ontario, for example, all existing acts of Canada or the provinces and territories are published. Each act includes all amendments made to it since the last publication. The volumes are published and are known as revised statutes (RS); and they are also identified by year, such as Revised Statutes of Canada 1985 (RSC 1985) and revised Statutes of Ontario 1990 (RSO 1990).

Citations consist of units, and there is a comma between each unit.

Each statute citation:

1. Starts with the name of the act (italicized):

    Family Law Act

2. Is followed by a comma:

    Family Law Act,

3. Lists the statute volume and the jurisdiction:

    RSO (Revised Statutes of Ontario)

4. Lists the year of the act:

    1990

5. Is followed by a comma:

    1990,

6. Lists any supplements or editions in brackets:

    (5th Supp)

    Note: Do not use superscripts.

    Note: Instead of using "nd" or "rd," as in 2nd or 3rd, use just "d" for either, such as 2d or 3d.

7. Is followed by a comma:

    (5th Supp),

8. Lists the chapter:

    c F.3

    Note: Chapters in Ontario use a period between the letter and number rather than a hyphen.

9. Is followed by a comma:

    c F.3,

10. Lists any sections or subsections, known as pinpoints:

    s 21

11. Ends in a period:

    Family Law Act, RSO 1990, c F.3, s 21.

Figure 1.14   Statute Citations

Title	Volume	Jurisdiction	Year	Chapter	Supplement	Pinpoint
Family Law Act,	RS	O	1990,	c F.3,		s 21.
Cited: *Family Law Act,* RSO 1990, c F.3, s 21.						
Criminal Code,	RS	C	1985,	c C-46,		s 745.
Cited: *Criminal Code,* RSC 1985, c C-46, s 745.						
Animal Pedigree Act,	RS	C	1985,	c 8	(5th Supp).	
Cited: *Animal Pedigree Act,* RSC 1985, c 8 (5th Supp).						

E. Regulations

Regulations are referred to as subordinate legislation since they are made under the authority of a statute; however, they are not created by Parliament or a legislature. They are created by departmental or ministry officials who have power to make regulations under the statute. They are the procedure or rules for administering that statute.

Regulations require, prohibit, or permit certain actions and set out a method of doing what is required or permitted. They also create penalties for not doing what is required or for doing what is prohibited.

Regulations, like statutes, are written in units with a comma between each unit.

Federal regulations are divided into two categories: revised (or re-enacted) and unrevised.

1. Revised or re-enacted regulations are listed as CRC (Consolidated Regulations of Canada), following the name of the regulation. The year of the revision is optional, but it is usually not included:

   Defence Clothing and Equipment Loan Order, CRC, c 686.

2. Unrevised regulations are listed as SOR (Statutory Orders and Regulations), following the name of the regulation. The year is listed first before the regulation number:

   Private Buoy Regulations, SOR/99-335.

   After the year 2000, four digits are used - e.g., 2010-336.

Provincial and territorial regulations are cited by name of regulation, jurisdiction, regulation number, and year.

As with federal regulations, there are two categories: revised and unrevised.

1. For revised regulations, the year is not repeated after the regulation number:

   Licences to Sell Liquor, RRO 1990, Reg 719.

2. For unrevised regulations, the regulation number is followed by the year. If the year is 2000 or later, four digits are used rather than two in most provinces. In Ontario, two digits are used.

Licences to Sell Liquor, O Reg 354/07.

Figure 1.15   Regulation Citations

Jurisdiction	Unrevised	Revised or Re-enacted
Canada	SOR	CRC
Provincial	O Reg	RRO

Cited:

Aircraft Objects Regulations, SOR/2008-109.
Air Cushion Vehicle Regulations, CRC, c 4.
Bare Land Strata Regulations, BC Reg 75/78.

F. Case Law

Case law is also referred to as jurisprudence, and comprises the decisions made by judges at various levels in the court system.

Cases can be published or unpublished. When they are published, they appear in reporters, periodicals, and yearbooks.

Citing methods become more complicated at this point, as there are neutral citations without punctuation, and parallel citations with punctuation. Also, there is the use of round and square brackets.

Citations do not include words such as et al; cite only the first party. Do not include periods after initials or abbreviations for incorporated business names.

1. NEUTRAL CITATIONS

Neutral citations are assigned to each case as decisions are made. You should not create one if one is not available. Neutral citations are a new naming method to identify a case, and they are not dependent upon a case being published in a report.

You can differentiate a neutral citation from a published one in that it refers to the court and not the reporter where the case was published.

Example of Neutral Citation:

MacLellan v MacLellan, **2001 NBCA 82.**

a. Title of proceeding:

MacLellan v MacLellan

b. Year of decision:

2001

c. Name of court:

New Brunswick Court of Appeal

d. Decision number:

82

Figure 1.16　Neutral Citation Rules

First Citation with Neutral Citation	Parallel Citation
R v Sharpe, 2001 SCC 2, [2001] 1 SCR 45	194 DLR (4th) 1
Cited: *R v Sharpe*, 2001 SCC 2, [2001] 1 SCR 45, 194 DLR (4th) 1.	

2. PARALLEL CITATION

Parallel citations are additional citations for an opinion that is published in more than one place, such as the Supreme Court cases and the Ontario Reports.

Court names are required if it is not obvious which court heard the case. Court names are not required for Supreme Court cases because it is obvious that it is the Supreme Court of Canada. They are also not required when neutral citations are used.

When the jurisdiction is obvious, the province or territory does not need to be included in the court name. For example, if the citation is reported in the Ontario Reports (OR), then the court can be (CA) for Court of Appeal, rather than (Ont CA) for Ontario Court of Appeal.

Never just include a neutral citation; always search for a published citation, perhaps using Quicklaw or Westlaw. Also, you are not required to cite all parallel citations. Your employer may direct you to select the official reporters such as the Federal Court Reports and Supreme Court Reports, semi-official reporters such as Ontario Reports, or perhaps Dominion Law Reports, which is an unofficial reporter.

Your professor will provide you with instructions for the preferred method. Be consistent when keying your citations. In a law firm, you will also be instructed on the method of presentation.

Case citations appear in the following order:

Figure 1.17　Case Citations

1.	Titles of proceedings, legislation, and regulations are italicized	*Dhillon v Dhillon* *R v Latimer* *Family Law Act* *Criminal Records Regulations*
2.	Square brackets [ ] 　Year is essential: indicates the year the 　decision was reported and is necessary 　to locate case	

3.	Round brackets ( ) Year is not essential: indicates the year the decision was made but is not necessary to locate case	
4.	Comma after title of proceeding and before square brackets	*R v Jackson*, [1993]
5.	Comma after title of proceeding and round brackets	*R v Westergard* (2004),
6.	Reporters: no spaces after periods within the reporter	OR SCR
7.	Court names are in round brackets	(CA) (SC)
8.	Series or Supplements Series: ordinal numeral (no superscript) in round brackets Supplements: abbreviation capitalized in round brackets	(1st) (2d) (3d) (4th) (Supp)
9.	Additional Abbreviations Chapter Section, subsection Sections, subsections Paragraph(s) And others (Latin) Schedule	 c s ss para(s) et al Sch
10.	Sequence of Case Law (see citation below) Title of proceeding (Year of decision) [Year of reporter] Volume Reporter Series (if any) Page Jurisdiction or court (if required)	 *Hemingway v Smith* (1983), 1 Dominion Law Reports (4th) 205 (British Columbia Court of Appeal)
	Hemingway v Smith (1983), 1 DLR (4th) 205 (BC CA).	
11.	Sequence of Legislation (see citation below) Title Statute volume Jurisdiction Year (Session or supplement) Chapter Pinpoint	 *Criminal Code* Revised Statutes Canada 1985 C-45 section 745, subsection 1
	Criminal Code, RSC 1985, c C-45, s 745(1).	

12.	Pinpoint Citation with Parallel Citation with Name of Judge	
	Title of proceeding	*R v Sharpe,*
	(Year of decision)	
	[Year of reporter]	[2001]
	Volume	1
	Reporter	Supreme Court Reports
	Series (if any)	
	Page	45
	Pinpoint	at 97
	Jurisdiction or court (if required)	Supreme Court of Canada (SCC)
	(year of decision)	
	[year of reporter]	
	Volume	194
	Reporter	Dominion Law Reports
	Series (if any)	(4th)
	Page	1
	Judge	, McLachlin (Chief Justice of Canada)
	R v Sharpe, [2001] 1 SCR 45 at 97, 194 DLR (4th) 1, McLachlin CJC	
13.	Neutral citation: appears after title of proceeding with no punctuation	2001 SCC 2
	R v Sharpe, 2001 SCC 2, [2001] 1 SCR 45 at 97, 194 DLR (4th) 1, McLachlin CJC	

Figure 1.18   Case Law Citation Order

Title of proceeding,
Neutral citation,
[Year of reporter]
Volume
Reporter
(Series)
Page
(Court).

or

Title of proceeding,
[Year of reporter]
Volume
Reporter
(Series)
Page
(Court).

or

Title of proceeding
(Year of decision),
Volume
Reporter
(Series)
Page
(Court).

or

Title of proceeding,
Neutral citation,
Volume
Reporter
(Series)
Page
(Court).

or

Title of proceeding,
Neutral citation,
First citation,
Parallel citation.
(Judge optional)

Figure 1.19   Case Law Citation Order

Title of Proceeding	(Year of Decision)	Neutral Citation	[Year of Reporter]	Volume	Reporter	(Series)	Page	(Court)
Hickey v Hickey,			[1999]	2	SCR		518.	
R v Barr	(1982),			16	Man R	(2d)	1	(Co Ct).
R v Nette,		2001 SCC 78,	[2001]	3	SCR		488.	

3. CANLII CITATIONS

CanLII citations are electronic and complement the neutral citation for the case. The citation has the following components:

a. *Title of proceeding*

b. The year of decision

c. CanLII identifier

d. Case number

e. Name of court

No punctuation is used, as in a neutral citation.

Example:

> *Malamas v Stanoulis*, **2009 CanLII 2321**

If there is a neutral citation, it is used and CanLII is in brackets.

Example:

> *317326 Alberta Ltd v Competition Chevrolet Oldsmobile Ltd,*
> **2004 ABCA 38 (CanLII).**

Note: You should avoid citing with CanLII unless the case is not available through any other publisher.

G. Abbreviations

Citations use abbreviations. The following abbreviations are based on the McGill method of citation. The tables are not complete and contain the abbreviations required for completing the assigned exercises.

1. PROVINCIAL AND TERRITORIAL

Figure 1.20   Provincial and Territorial Abbreviations

Province/Territory	Statutes	Regulations	Courts	Neutral Citations	Law Reporters
Alberta	A	Alta	Alta	AB	A or Alta
British Columbia	BC	BC	BC	BC	BC
Manitoba	M	Man	Man	MB	Man
New Brunswick	NB	NB	NB	NB	NB
Newfoundland and Labrador	NL	NL	Nfld	NL	Nfld
Northwest Territories	NWT	NWT	NWT	NWT	NWT
Nova Scotia	NS	NS	NS	NS	NS
Nunavut	Nu	Nu	Nu	NU	Nu

Province/Territory	Statutes	Regulations	Courts	Neutral Citations	Law Reporters
Ontario	O	O	Ont	ON	O
Prince Edward Island	PEI	PEI	PEI	PE	PEI
Quebec	Q	Q	Qc	QC	Q
Saskatchewan	S	S	Sask	SK	Sask
Yukon	Y	Y	Y	YK	Y

2. COURT NAMES

Figure 1.21   Court Name Abbreviations

(Gen Div)	General Division
(Prov Div)	Provincial Division
CA	Court of Appeal
Ct J	Court of Justice
FC	Federal Court
FCA	Federal Court of Appeal
HC	High Court
Prov Ct	Provincial Court
QB	Court of Queen's Bench
SCC	Supreme Court of Canada
Sup Ct	Superior Court
TCC	Tax Court of Canada

3. JUDICIAL NAMES

Figure 1.22   Judicial Name Abbreviations

CJ	Chief Justice
CJA	Chief Justice of Appeal
CJC	Chief Justice of Canada
J	Judge/Justice
JA	Judge/Justice of Appeal
JJ	Judges/Justices
JJA	Judges/Justices of Appeal
Mag	Magistrate

4. STATUTES

Figure 1.23   Statute Abbreviations

CRC	Consolidated Regulations of Canada
RR + Provincial regulation abbreviation (RRO)	Revised Regulations
RS + Provincial statute abbreviation (RSO)	Revised Statutes
RSC	Revised Statutes of Canada
S + Provincial statute abbreviation (SO)	Statute
SC	Statutes of Canada

5. REPORTERS/PERIODICALS/YEARBOOKS

Figure 1.24   Reporter, Periodical, and Yearbook Abbreviations

Provincial reporter abbreviation + AC (OAC)	Appeal Cases
ACWS	All Canada Weekly Summaries
BLR	Business Law Reports
CBR	Canadian Bankruptcy Reports
CCC	Canadian Criminal Cases
CCEL	Canadian Cases on Employment Law
CHRR	Canadian Human Rights Reporter
CPR	Canadian Patent Reporter
CR	Criminal Reports
CTC	Canadian Tax Cases
DLR	Dominion Law Reports
FC	Federal Court Reports
LAC	Labour Arbitration Cases
Provincial reporter abbreviation + LR (OLR)	Law Report
NR	National Reporter
Provincial reporter abbreviation + R (OR)	Reports
RFL	Reports of Family Law
SCR	Supreme Court Reports
WN	Weekly Notes
WWR	Western Weekly Reports

Glossary Term Definitions

Express Scribe   free, downloadable software used to listen to voice files while transcribing them in a separate word-processing software

floater   an administrative staff member who "floats" around the firm in different administrative positions, usually to fill in for staff that are sick or on vacation; also works on overflow duties when a particular staff member has more work than can be done by one person

hot keys   keystrokes or keystroke combinations that cause specific reactions for a specific software

keyboard shortcuts   see "hot keys" above

CHAPTER 2
General Administration

I. INTRODUCTION

In this chapter, we will focus on transcription tasks that you may be given that do not relate to a specific area of law. You may work in a large law firm for a lawyer who practises a specific area of law, or you may work in a smaller firm that practises many areas of law. In either case, there are often times when you may be asked to transcribe something that is not area or file specific. Some examples of these scenarios are:

1. Internal and external memos:

   a. Regarding **conflict of interest**, where lawyers generally avoid representing both sides of a file or court action, so as not to compromise their client's position

   b. To the accounting department

   c. To other lawyers

   d. To Human Resources (department within the law firm that handles employee-related tasks such as hiring, interviewing, firing, and disciplinary matters) regarding holidays, benefits, sick leave, salary expectations, performance evaluations (an annual review of an employee's performance at work), to name a few

   e. To department heads regarding departmental issues

   f. To IT regarding computer and software challenges

   g. To articling students (individuals who have completed their law degree and need work experience in order to be called to the bar) regarding research or other projects

   h. To **title searchers** (individuals who perform searches involving the research of documents and plans concerning a parcel of land) regarding work to be done

   i. To **process servers** (individuals retained by law firms to serve court documents on opposing parties) regarding documentation to be served

2. **Flat, or block, fee accounts** in situations where a lawyer does not want to use the account produced by the firm's accounting software. These accounts are generally where a lawyer charges a set amount for work done on a client's file. The amount is the same regardless of the amount of time it takes to complete the work.

3. Volunteer work to be done by a lawyer that is not file specific, such as presentations to classes, potential clients, and articles for industry publications or newspapers - the *Canadian Journal of Law and Society*, for example

4. Content for the firm's website

5. Email messages to be sent from a lawyer's email account in cases where the lawyer is not computer savvy but wants to communicate electronically or in cases where the message will be lengthy

6. Voice mail messages left by clients, lawyers, or other interested parties with respect to either

   a. open (ongoing client files that the firm is currently working on)

   b. closed (files that have been completed and sent to a storage facility for safe keeping) or

   c. potential client files (files that may become open files, if it is found that accepting the file will not result in a conflict of interest)

   These voice mail messages are usually transcribed - a lawyer will listen to the message and forward it to an assistant's voice mail with instructions to transcribe it.

7. Correspondence:

   a. To one-time clients - these types of clients typically walk into the law firm requesting work to be done immediately - examples of requests of this nature would be swearing affidavits, signing passport applications, and reviewing documentation from other law firms in other cities or countries

   b. To various businesses and professional organizations not related to a particular file - examples may include advertisements, office supplies, various services, publications for the law library, subscriptions (ongoing receipt of a certain publication) for the firm's waiting room, and registrations for upcoming seminars (periodic legal professional development courses)

A. Glossary Term Definitions

conflict of interest	occurs when opposing parties are represented by the same law firm
flat fee/block fee accounts	all-inclusive set fees for legal services performed
process server	individual who delivers court documents to parties named on documents
title searcher	individual who searches property for ownership and other claims filed against the property

II. TERMINOLOGY EXERCISE

A. **Fill in the blanks using the correct terminology found in the chapter introduction:**

1. Working in a law firm can be very exciting. Lawyers meet with clients to decide whether or not they will _____ a file for the client. This is determined after the firm performs a search to see whether it has ever represented the opposing party. The firm is searching for a _____ of _____. Once the work on a client's file is completed, the firm sends the client an account. If the lawyer is charging a set fee or _____ fee, the amount will be the same regardless of the amount of time it takes to complete the work. Work on a client's file can be done by lawyers, legal assistants, law clerks, or _____, who are students hired out of law school that have yet to be called to the bar. Once the client pays the account, the file is _____ and sent to a storage area.

2. When working in a firm as a legal assistant, you may be required to sign a lawyer up for a _____, where the lawyer will attend an industry-specific educational event. You may also be required to order _____ such as paper clips and staples. You may be responsible to maintain the firm's magazine _____ for journals such as the *Canadian Journal of Law and Society*.

III. CITATION EXERCISE

A. Rewrite each of the following by putting the units in the correct order with the correct punctuation:

1. RSC 1985

    Canadian Human Rights Act

    c H-6

    _____

2. *Canada Labour Code*

    c L-2

    RSC 1985

    _____

3. *Canada Labour Standards Regulations*

    CRC

    c 986

    _____

4. NS Reg 198

    Health Hazards Regulations

    2005

    _____

5. *Human Rights Code*

    RSBC 1996

    c 210

    _____

6. *Occupational Health and Safety Regulation*

    296/97

    BC Reg

    _____

7. SS 1993

   Occupational Health and Safety Act, 1993

   c O-1.1

   _____

8. *Machtinger v HOJ Industries Ltd*

   [1992]

   986 (page)

   1 (volume)

   SCR

   _____

9. *Wallace v United Grain Growers Ltd*

   [1997]

   3 (volume)

   SCR

   701 (page)

   _____

10. [1991]

    Canada (Human Rights Commission) v Sun Life Assurance Co of Canada

    3 (volume)

    SCR

    689 (page)

    _____

B. Rewrite each of the following citations by fixing all errors in formatting, spacing, and punctuation:

1. *Canada (Human Rights Commission) v. Canadian Airlines International Ltd.*, 2006 S.C.C. 1,[2006] 1 S.C.R. 3.

_____

2. *Occupational Health and Safety Act*, R.S.A. 2000, c.O-2.

_____

3. *Workplace Safety and Insurance Act*, 1997,S.O. 1997, c. 16, Sch. A.

_____

4. *Canada Occupational Health and Safety Regulations*, SOR/86-304.

_____

5. Hemingway v. Smith (1983), 1 D.L.R. (4th) 205 (BC C.A.).

_____

6. *Sills v. Children's Aid Society of the City of Belleville*, (2001)53 O.R. (3) 577, 198 DLR (4th) 485 (C.A.).

_____

7. *Allied Adjusters & Co. Ltd. v. Sihikalo* (1981), 26 BCLR 363, (C.A.).

_____

8. *Komarnicki v. Hurricane Hydrocarbons Ltd.*, 2007 ABQB 60, 56 C.C.E.L. (3rd) 203.

_____

9. Haley v. Air Canada (1999), 177 N.S.R. (2) 400 (C.A.).

_____

10. *Labour Standards Act*, RSS 1978, c. L-1.

_____

IV. PUNCTUATION RULES: COMMAS

A. Introductory Clauses

There is always a comma at the end of an introductory clause for sentences starting with:

1. In
2. On
3. After
4. As
5. If
6. Should
7. Having
8. To
9. Before
10. Because
11. Although
12. Even though
13. For
14. Unless
15. Until
16. When
17. Where
18. While

B. Conjunctions

There is also always a comma in the following circumstances:

1. , but + complete sentence
2. , and + complete sentence
3. , or + complete sentence

C. Introductory Words or Transitional Expressions

You will always find a comma after the following words:

1. However,

2. Therefore,

3. Yes,

A comma is also inserted both before and after the following transitional words:

1. , however,

2. , therefore,

D. Geography and Dates

1. There is always a comma between the name of a city and the name of a province - there is also always a comma after the name of the province:

    Toronto, Ontario,

2. There is a comma after the day in a written date - the year always has a comma on either side of it:

    On September 11, 20xx,

3. There is no comma between the month and year, if there is no day written:

    In September 20xx, we were …

4. There is no comma after a month and day, where no year is indicated:

    Please come over on September 12 to see my new office.

E. Non-Essential Expressions, Words, or Phrases

There is, no doubt, a good reason why our client wants to plead guilty.

Our receptionist, Collette, was the one who opened the door.

F. Interrupting Elements

We can file the notice of motion today or, if you wish, tomorrow.

G. Afterthoughts

It's not too late, is it?

H. Quotations

, "I think that …"

I. Academic Degrees

There is a comma before and after an academic degree:

David A. Stout, LL.B.,

J. Series

There is a comma before the *and/or* in a series of three or more items:

one, two, and three

apples, oranges, or bananas

K. With Adjectives

A comma replaces the word *and* when using two adjectives:

Tracy is a generous, outgoing person.

L. Words of Direct Address

You know, Ms. Jones, I am very capable of doing that assignment.

M. Telephone Numbers

Please call me at 613-727-4723, ext. 5870.

V. PUNCTUATION EXERCISE: COMMAS

A. **Are the following sentences punctuated correctly? Answer true (T) if the sentence properly uses a comma and false (F) if it does not.**

1. ___ You have now completed your first month here, and I would like to congratulate you on working at Justice Canada.

2. ___ The order for lunch at the seminar includes sandwiches, juice, coffee and water.

3. ___ Joanne has proven to be a dedicated, responsible Managing Partner.

4. ___ If it is necessary we will hold training sessions for the new Microsoft Suite.

5. ___ My aunt Ruth, who lives in Amherst, Nova Scotia, is retired.

6. ___ Michel Asselin, P. Eng, was the keynote speaker.

7. ___ You see, Ms. Payne, I do intend to complete my work, but it requires me to work overtime this weekend.

8. ___ The technician, who installed the new telephone system is the only one who can answer your question.

9. ___ We knew that, late or not, we were expected to attend the corporate law workshop.

10. ___ The person at the Registry Office whom you saw yesterday was Robert Read.

11. ___ Yes we can accommodate your holiday request.

12. ___ We can accommodate you on October 19, should you wish to attend.

13. ___ Ask the staff Mr. Charles if they are planning to stay for the reception.

14. ___ Rich declared "This is the best law firm ever!"

15. ___ As soon as you finish this file we will start your next file.

16. ___ Come and see me on Monday to talk about your performance evaluation.

17. ___ Will they be staying at the Lord Elgin Hotel, or will they be staying at the Embassy Suites?

18. ___ Furthermore please take time this weekend to have some fun.

19. ___ The fact that you are going to graduate this spring, however, does not mean that you should not continue your learning.

20. ___ We arranged for another appointment but they will be out of town on September 30.

VI. BEGINNER VOICE FILES

A. Beginner Voice File 1

Voice file: docs > CH2 > ch2beg1.mp3

Word template: docs > templates > memo.doc

Instructions: This is an interoffice memorandum. Use the interoffice memorandum template above or a template provided by your professor.

B. Beginner Voice File 2

Voice file: docs > CH2 > ch2beg2.mp3

Word template: docs > templates > letter.doc

Instructions: This is a letter. Use the letter template above or a template provided by your professor.

C. Beginner Voice File 3

Voice file: docs > CH2 > ch2beg3.mp3

Word template: docs > templates > memo.doc

Instructions: This is an interoffice memorandum. Use the interoffice memorandum template above or a template provided by your professor.

VII. INTERMEDIATE VOICE FILES

A. Intermediate Voice File 1

Voice file: docs > CH2 > ch2int1.mp3

Word template: docs > templates > memo.doc

Instructions: This is an interoffice memorandum. Use the interoffice memorandum template above or a template provided by your professor.

B. Intermediate Voice File 2

Voice file: docs > CH2 > ch2int2.mp3

Word template: docs > templates > memo.doc

Instructions: This is an interoffice memorandum. Use the interoffice memorandum template above or a template provided by your professor.

C. Intermediate Voice File 3

Voice file: docs > CH2 > ch2int3.mp3

Word template: docs > templates > letter.doc

Instructions: This is a letter. Use the letter template above or a template provided by your professor.

VIII. ADVANCED VOICE FILES

A. Advanced Voice File 1

Voice file: docs > CH2 > ch2adv1.mp3

Word template: docs > templates > memo.doc

Instructions: This is an interoffice memorandum. Use the interoffice memorandum template above or a template provided by your professor.

B. Advanced Voice File 2

Voice file: docs > CH2 > ch2adv2.mp3

Word template: docs > templates > memo.doc

Instructions: This is an interoffice memorandum. Use the interoffice memorandum template above or a template provided by your professor.

C. Advanced Voice File 3

Voice file: docs > CH2 > ch2adv3.mp3

Word template: docs > templates > account.doc

Instructions: This is a statement of account. Use the statement of account template above or a template provided by your professor.

CHAPTER 3
Wills and Powers of Attorney

I. INTRODUCTION

In this chapter, we will focus on transcription tasks within the legal areas of drafting last will and testaments and powers of attorney. Most law firms offer these services to their clients, and clients come into the office to have both prepared at the same time in order to ensure their affairs are in order. It provides great peace of mind. As well, banks and trust companies may also offer this service to their clients through their estate departments.

A. Last Will and Testament

A **last will and testament** is a legal document that is prepared by the **testator** to outline his wishes on death in terms of the distribution of his **estate**. A female testator may be referred to as a testatrix. The estate comprises both **real property** and **personal property**. Real property is real estate, and personal property is all property other than real estate. Personal property is also referred to as chattels.

An **executor** is named as the person designated to look after distribution of the estate after the death of the testator. A female executor may be referred to as an executrix. More than one person may be named as the executors of the estate.

If **minor** children are involved (children under the age of 18), the testator will name a **guardian**, who is the person requested to care for the minor children. A **trustee** will also be named, and this person will be responsible for the financial affairs on behalf of the minor children. Normally the guardian and trustee are the same person.

The testator will list **beneficiaries** of the estate and may outline fixed amounts and/or percentages of the estate to be received.

One clause that is very common to include in a will is a ***per stirpes*** clause that will entitle the heirs of a beneficiary to receive property through the last will and testament should the beneficiary be deceased when it comes time to carry out the wishes of the testator.

A will must be signed by two **witnesses** who are both present and can attest to the testator signing the document.

There are several ways to change a will: One is to completely rewrite the will; another is to initial any minor changes on both sides of the changes; and still another is to prepare a **codicil**, whereby a new legal document is created and attached to the last will and testament outlining a minor change, such as a different executor, guardian, trustee, beneficiary, or amount of distribution.

B. Powers of Attorney

Powers of attorney give authority to others to act on someone's behalf when they are unable to do so. This may be because he is deemed **mentally incompetent**, which means he cannot understand the consequences of his decisions, or it may be that he will be out of the country and require someone to conduct his financial affairs on his behalf.

Many provinces divide powers of attorney into two separate legal documents. One document is for property purposes and the other is for personal care; however, some lawyers use one document to cover both purposes.

In Ontario, the document for financial purposes is called a **continuing power of attorney for property**. It can be used immediately after it is executed. This document grants wide-ranging authority if there are no restrictions outlined. The person giving the authority to another person to act is the **grantor**. Another common name used is donor. Depending on the province, the name of the person creating a power of attorney may differ as it directly relates to the forms of that province.

The person who is given the power to act on the grantor's behalf is called the **attorney**. You may see this person referred to as the grantee or donee. The attorney is granted the ability to undertake financial dealings such as withdrawing funds from your bank account or selling your home. Each province has its own name for this type of power of attorney. For instance, in British Columbia, it is called an "enduring power of attorney."

In Ontario, the document for personal care is called a **power of attorney for personal care**. Again, each province names its documents differently, so always check the provincial legislation.

Powers of attorney are usually, but not always, arranged well in advance of their use and come into effect only when certain conditions are met. An example would be a power of attorney for property coming into effect only while the grantor is out of the country, and would, therefore, cease to be in effect on her return. The powers of attorney require the signature of two **witnesses** who must be over the age of 18. Both the witnesses and the grantor **execute** the documents in front of each other.

You can **revoke** your powers of attorney at any time in writing. This will cancel the authority you have given to the attorney.

C. Glossary Term Definitions

attorney/grantee/donee	person who is given authority over assets or personal care by the grantor
beneficiaries	people named in a will to receive property as a result of the will
codicil	legal document making minor changes to a will
continuing power of attorney for property	tends to financial matters and is to be used when grantor is rendered unable to act on behalf of himself or herself
estate	assets on death (real and personal property)
execute	sign a document
executor/executrix	person named in a will to administer and distribute the estate
grantor/donor	person granting authority to attorney to act on his or her behalf in regard to assets or personal care
guardian	person named in a will to have the authority to care for the testator's minor children
last will and testament (will)	legal document outlining one's wishes on death in terms of distribution of estate
mentally incompetent	unable to understand the consequences of one's decisions
minor	child under the age of 18
per stirpes	clause in a will that entitles heirs of a beneficiary to receive property in the event of a beneficiary's death
personal property	chattels or all property other than real estate, including bank accounts, investments, and valuable items
power of attorney for personal care	tends to health-care needs and is to be used when grantor is rendered unable to act on behalf of himself or herself
powers of attorney	legal devices giving authority to others to act on one's behalf
real property	real estate
revoke	cancel the authority
testator/testatrix	person making a will
trustee	person given the authority to administer assets on behalf of a third party; for example, minor children
witnesses	people over the age of 18 who validate that the document was properly executed

II. TERMINOLOGY EXERCISE

A. **Fill in the blanks using the correct terminology found in the chapter introduction:**

1. Susy has decided that she would like to have her wishes known on her death. She has to create a legal document that is called a _____. This document distributes her property on her death. She has been advised that her property is known as her _____ in terms of her assets on death.

2. An estate consists of two types of property, which are _____ and _____.

3. Susy is called the _____ in this document because she is the one creating it. The person she assigns to look after the distribution of her estate is called the _____.

4. If she has minor children, she will name a person to care for them. This person is called the _____.

5. She would also name a person to look after the finances of the minor children, and this person is called the _____. Minor children are those children under the age of _____.

6. The people she names in the last will and testament to receive gifts as a result of her death are called the _____.

7. There is a clause she can use in her last will and testament to ensure that the heirs of her beneficiaries will receive an entitlement in the event of a beneficiary being deceased at the time the will is distributed. This clause is referred to as a _____ clause.

8. If Susy wishes to make a change to her last will and testament without creating a new will, she can create a _____, which makes minor changes.

B. **Fill in the blanks using the correct terminology found in the chapter introduction:**

1. Susy also wants to give someone authority to make decisions on her behalf, so she has asked a lawyer to prepare her _____.

2. She is called the _____ and the person given the authority is called the _____.

3. The authority will not be used until particular conditions are met; for example, if Susy is deemed _____, which means she cannot understand the consequences of her decisions. The following two powers of attorney will be created: a _____ to look after her banking and other money-related matters, and a _____ to look after her accommodation, nutrition, medication, and other such requirements for her well-being when she is no longer able to do so for herself.

4. Powers of attorney require two _____ who must attest that she signed the document. At any point in time, Susy can _____ the authority, which cancels the powers.

III. CITATION EXERCISE

A. Rewrite each of the following by putting the units in the correct order with the correct punctuation:

1. c 30

    Substitute Decisions Act, 1992

    SO 1992

    _____

2. RSBC 1996

    Power of Attorney Act

    c 370

    _____

3. *Wills Act, 1996*

    SS 1996

    c W-14.1

    _____

4. O Reg 100/96

    Accounts and Records of Attorneys and Guardians

    _____

5. *Wills v Doe* (1992)

    90 (volume)

    DLR

    164 (page)

    (4th)

    (BC SC)

    _____

6. *Health Care Consent Act, 1996*

    c 2

    SO 1996

    Sch A

    _____

7. RSNB 1973

   Wills Act

   c W-9

---

8. *Probate Act*

   RSPEI 1988

   c P-21

---

9. RSO 1990

   Powers of Attorney Act

   c P.20

---

10. *Powers of Attorney Act, 2002*

    SS 2002

    c P-20.3

B. **Rewrite each of the following citations by fixing all errors in formatting, spacing, and punctuation:**

1. Powers of Attorney Act, R.S.O. 1990, c. P.20

    _____

2. *Trustee Act*, RSO 1990, c T.23.

    _____

3. *Succession Law Reform Act*, R.S.O 1990, c. S.26.

    _____

4. Powers of Attorney Act, R.S.A. 2000, c. P-20.

    _____

5. Wills Act, R.S.A. 2000, c. W-12

    _____

6. *Estate of Joseph Roy v. Mary Pimentel*, 2005 NBQB 229, 284 N.B.R. (2) 200

    _____

7. *R. v. Hunter*, 2008 O.N.C.A. 103, [2008] 3 CTC 248

    _____

8. Egli v. Egli, 2005 BCCA 627, 262 D.L.R. (4th) 208, (2005), 48 B.C.L.R. (4th) 90.

    _____

9. *Doherty v. Doherty* (1997), 190 NBR (2d) 303. (C.A.)

    _____

10. Wills Act, RSY 2002, c. 230

    _____

IV. PUNCTUATION RULES: PERIODS, QUESTION MARKS, AND EXCLAMATION MARKS

A. Period

1. Ends a sentence:

    The court recessed today.

2. Ends an indirect question (direction) where you do not expect an answer:

    Would you please deliver that file to Mr. McCoy today.

3. Used with abbreviations:

    Jr. or p.m.

B. Question Mark

For a direct question where you are expecting an answer:

Are you coming over for dinner tonight?

C. Exclamation Mark

Used to express surprise, shock, excitement, urgency, a strong feeling, or enthusiasm:

Oh!

We did it!

V. PUNCTUATION EXERCISE: PERIODS, QUESTION MARKS, AND EXCLAMATION MARKS

A. Complete each of the following sentences with the appropriate punctuation: period, question mark, or exclamation mark.

1. Will you be able to attend the corporate seminar on Friday

2. Are you in a position to work overtime this weekend

3. You do not have any client appointments today

4. Send me your draft affidavit as soon as possible

5. What a great idea

6. Would you please send me your report as soon as possible

7. I am sure you will agree we need to work on the Smith last will and testament immediately

8. Is your appointment Wednesday at 2 p.m.

9. Fantastic

10. May I have your draft divorce order by Friday

11. Would you be able to act as staff representative for this month's firm meeting

12. May I suggest that you review the client's instructions before you prepare the powers of attorney

13. You're hired

14. Would you arrange to have this year's speakers for the estate-planning session contact you directly with any concerns

15. Would you please call me if you need further assistance

16. Do you prefer to take lunch at noon or 1 p.m.

17. Please come and see me when you are finished meeting with the client

18. Are you away this Friday

19. Do you need a health-care directive

20. Incredible

VI. BEGINNER VOICE FILES

A. Beginner Voice File 1

Voice file: docs > CH3 > ch3beg1.mp3

Word template: docs > templates > letter.doc

Instructions: This is a letter. Use the letter template above or a template provided by your professor.

B. Beginner Voice File 2

Voice file: docs > CH3 > ch3beg2.mp3

Word template: docs > templates > letter.doc

Instructions: This is a letter. Use the letter template above or a template provided by your professor.

C. Beginner Voice File 3

Voice file: docs > CH3 > ch3beg3.mp3

Word template: docs > templates > voice.doc

Instructions: This is a voice message. Use the voice message template above or a template provided by your professor.

VII. INTERMEDIATE VOICE FILES

A. Intermediate Voice File 1

Voice file: docs > CH3 > ch3int1.mp3

Word template: docs > templates > voice.doc

Instructions: This is a voice message. Use the voice message template above or a template provided by your professor.

B. Intermediate Voice File 2

Voice file: docs > CH3 > ch3int2.mp3

Word template: docs > templates > voice.doc

Instructions: This is a voice message. Use the voice message template above or a template provided by your professor.

C. Intermediate Voice File 3

Voice file: docs > CH3 > ch3int3.mp3

Word template: docs > templates > letter.doc

Instructions: This is a letter. Use the letter template above or a template provided by your professor.

VIII. ADVANCED VOICE FILES

A. Advanced Voice File 1

Voice file: docs > CH3 > ch3adv1.mp3

Word template: docs > templates > letter.doc

Instructions: This is a letter. Use the letter template above or a template provided by your professor.

B. Advanced Voice File 2

Voice file: docs > CH3 > ch3adv2.mp3

Word template: docs > templates > letter.doc
                docs > templates > account.doc

Instructions: This is a letter and statement of account. Use the letter and statement of account template above or a template provided by your professor.

C. Advanced Voice File 3

Voice file: docs > CH3 > ch3adv3.mp3

Word template: docs > templates > will.doc

Instructions: These are instructions to complete a last will and testament precedent. Use the instructions to complete a last will and testament precedent template above or a template provided by your professor.

CHAPTER 4

Estates

I. INTRODUCTION

This chapter focuses on transcription tasks in the area of estate administration. An **estate** is one's property on death - both real and personal property. The client will arrive with a **last will and testament** (a "will") of a loved one, or if there is no last will and testament found, the client will be seeking guidance as to how to proceed.

Estate affairs are conducted by law firms as well as trust companies or trust departments of banks.

Estate administration is a process of having the will validated through the courts and having the estate distributed accordingly. The court process is called **probate**.

If a person dies with a will in place, the person is deemed to have died **testate** and the wishes of the deceased will be distributed according to the will. If a person dies without having created a will, or if a will cannot be found, the person has been deemed to have died **intestate** and **succession laws** will be consulted to determine which beneficiaries will inherit based on bloodlines or spousal relationships to the deceased. Property that is gifted through a will or succession is referred to as a **bequest**.

In order to carry out the wishes of the deceased, an **executor** has to be appointed through the courts to obtain authority to distribute the estate. In Ontario, we call the executor an **estate trustee** at this stage in the **application** to the court; however, the term executor will be used for our purposes.

Probate ensures that the last will and testament is legally valid, and the court approves the person who has applied to be the executor to distribute the estate. This is normally the person who was appointed as executor in the last will and testament to carry out the wishes of the **testator**.

Although the process is similar in all provinces, the legislation is different in each province as are the names of the court forms.

Most executors will **retain** a law firm to assist. The lawyers will complete the forms on behalf of the executor and apply to the court for probate. Executors do not have to obtain a lawyer to probate an estate; however, it is strongly recommended.

An Ontario form called a "notice of appointment of estate trustee with a will" is completed, outlining who the beneficiaries are that are entitled to receive under the will, the name of the deceased, and the name of the person applying to be the executor of the estate.

Application is filed with the court outlining the value of the estate and the name of the executor applying for approval to distribute the estate. In Ontario, this form is called an "application for certificate of appointment of an estate trustee with a will." A tax is payable at the time of the application to the court based on the value of the estate (real and personal property).

Once the court has reviewed the last will and testament, as well as the application for appointment of the estate trustee, a document approving the appointment is executed by the court. In Ontario, it is called the "certificate of appointment of estate trustee with a will, and in British Columbia, it is called "letters probate." Check the legislation and forms in each province and territory to ensure the correct terminology is being used.

Once the court has approved the executor, the estate can then be disbursed according to the wishes of the deceased. Such responsibilities of the executor may include closing bank accounts, transferring or selling property, cashing in life insurance policies, cashing in stocks and bonds, paying the funeral expenses, and paying any debts of the deceased.

Frequently, an executor will hand off many responsibilities of the estate administration to a law firm or trust company because he or she may lack the expertise or emotional capacity to perform the associated tasks.

A **notarial certificate** is a form created by the law firm authenticating that the document attached to it is an exact duplicate of the original. Because there is only one original document authorizing the appointment of the executor, the original is kept on file and copies are sent out to insurance companies, banks, and other institutions in order to prove that the executor has the authority to administer the estate. Many notarial certificates will be prepared to serve this purpose.

Sometimes there is opposition to the appointment of the executor and the estate's distribution. All beneficiaries have the right to contest the appointment of the person applying to distribute the estate. After appointment of the executor, the distribution of the estate cannot be completed until all beneficiaries have signed a **waiver** releasing the executor from any further responsibility. Distributing an estate can take two to three years or longer.

A. Glossary Term Definitions

application	court document and process of applying for probate and appointment of estate trustee
bequest	property gifted through a will or succession
estate	assets on death (real and personal property)
estate trustee	court-appointed person authorized to distribute estate in Ontario
executor	court-appointed person authorized to distribute an estate
intestate	condition arising when someone dies without a valid will
last will and testament (will)	legal document outlining one's wishes on death in terms of distribution of property
notarial certificate	legal document authenticating that the attached document is an exact duplicate of the original
probate	court process of validating last will and testament and appointing an estate trustee
retain	to hire a law firm for representation
succession laws	set of laws that use spousal relationships or bloodlines to determine heirs and the distribution of assets in cases where an individual dies intestate
testate	condition arising when one dies with a valid will in place
testator/testatrix	person making a will
waiver	legal document releasing the estate trustee of further obligations to the estate

II. TERMINOLOGY EXERCISE

A. **Fill in the blanks using the terminology found in the introduction:**

1. Susy has passed away as a result of her car accident injuries. Her sister, Samatha, knew she was named as her executor and knew where to locate the _____,which outlined her sister's wishes on death. Because Susy had a will, and because the original will was found, she is deemed to have died _____ in the eyes of the court. Had Susy's last will and testament not been found, she would have been deemed to have died _____ and, therefore, the estate would have to be distributed according to _____, whereby her heirs would receive a bequest as a result.

2. Samantha has taken the will to their family lawyer. The law firm will now start the _____ process through the courts. Samantha is now called the _____ on the court forms, which means she will be the person who will be responsible for the distribution of the estate. To obtain the court's permission, an _____ must be filed through a series of documents prepared by the law firm.

3. The court has now approved Samantha to distribute the estate. She has decided to _____ the services of the law firm, because she is distraught and doesn't feel able to deal with the legal tasks at hand.

4. The law firm has obtained the court document authorizing the appointment of the estate trustee. Distribution can now begin. To prove this authorization, _____ are prepared and attached to copies of the original court document.

5. Samantha is aware that she has to have a _____ signed by each beneficiary before she can be released from her duties.

B. **Answer true or false to each of the following:**

1. ___ If a last will and testament is not found, the estate is considered testate.

2. ___ Probate is the process of preparing a last will and testament.

3. ___ If a person dies intestate, the estate is distributed according to bloodlines.

4. ___ The court does not approve the appointment of the executor; it only validates the last will and testament as being authentic.

5. ___ Completed notarial certificates are prepared by the courthouse and mailed to the law firms.

6. ___ The appointment of an executor can be disputed by the beneficiaries.

7. ___ One of the executor's responsibilities is to transfer property to the beneficiaries if it is willed this way.

8. ___ Only law firms can be retained to apply for probate.

9. ___ Estate legislation in Canada is the same in each province.

10. ___ Probate document names vary by province.

III. CITATION EXERCISE

A. Rewrite each of the following by putting the units in the correct order with the correct punctuation:

1. CRC

    Veterans Estates Regulations

    c 1584

    _____

2. c E.21

    RSO 1990

    Estates Act

    _____

3. *Administration of Estates Act*

    RSA 2000

    c A-2

    _____

4. RSA 2000

    Intestate Succession Act

    c I-10

    _____

5. *Dieno Estate v Dieno Estate*

    147 (volume)

    Sask R

    14 (page)

    [1996]

    10 (volume)

    WWR

    375 (page)

    (QB)

    _____

6. RSS 1978

   c M-31

   Municipal Industrial Development Corporations Act

---

7. 142 (volume)

   Man R

   (2d)

   119 (page)

   Jumelle v Soloway Estate

   (1999)

   (CA)

---

8. c E-13

   Executors and Trustees Act

   RSNB 1973

---

9. *Mitchell Estate v Mitchell Estate*

   (2004)

   228 (volume)

   NSR

   (2d)

   295 (page)

   2004 NSCA 149

---

10. *Estate Actions Act*

    c 152

    RSNS 1989

B. Rewrite each of the following citations by fixing all errors in formatting, spacing, and punctuation:

1. *Estates Regulations*, CRC, c. 1048.

_____

2. *Dundee Estates Limited Sale Authorization Order*, S.O.R./90-430

_____

3. R. v Caron, 2009 ABCA 34, 446 A.R. 362.

_____

4. *Settled Estates Ltd. v. Minister of National Revenue* [1960], SCR 606.

_____

5. *United Estates Ltd. v. Kennedy et al.*, [1940] S.C.R. 625

_____

6. *Boozary Estate*, (2005) 18 C.B.R. (5th) 205 (ON. S.C.).

_____

7. Burke Estate v. Burke Estate (1994), 7 R.F.L.(4th) 114 (Ont. S.C.).

_____

8. *Estate Administration Act*, RSBC. 1996, c. 122.

_____

9. *Serdahely Estate*, 2002 ABQB 10, 309 AR 370.

_____

10. *Ladner Estate*, 2001 BCSC 943, 27 C.B.R. (4th) 82.

_____

IV. PUNCTUATION RULES: SEMICOLONS AND COLONS

1. Semicolon

   a. Separates two complete sentences of the same thought, whereby the semicolon replaces the conjunction "and"

   b. Used between units where multiple commas are used

   c. Used before a transition word where two sentences are of the same thought such as

      ; however,

2. Colon

   a. Used in a sentence before a listing - the first letter is not capitalized if it is not a complete sentence

      We need new supplies: pens and pencils.

   b. Used in a list that is double spaced after the colon and enumerations are used and the first letters of the list are capitalized

      We need new supplies:
      1. **Pens**
      2. **Pencils**
      3. **Paper clips**

   c. Used with the following words:

      is/are as follows:

      are these:

      If you are not using these terms, then just complete a normal sentence without a colon, such as:

      The courses we are taking are Legal Document Production and Executive Integrated Projects

   d. Used in time:

      2:45 p.m. or 14:45

      Note: The 24-hour clock does not use a colon.

      1300 hours

   e. After the word "note," use a colon followed by a capital letter:

      Note: It is time to register for the conference.

V. PUNCTUATION EXERCISE: SEMICOLONS AND COLONS

A. **Select the correct answer for each of the following:**

1. There are a few things left to do this year, which are as follows we have to plan your graduation, and we have to plan a career event.

   a) Semicolon after *follows*

   b) Colon after follows and a capital letter on *we*

   c) Colon after *follows*

   d) No changes

2. Today we are working on proofreading it is your favourite thing to do.

   a) Semicolon after *proofreading*

   b) Colon after *proofreading*

   c) No changes

3. We are going to visit Paris, France, Dublin, Ireland, London, England, and Zurich, Switzerland.

   a) Semicolons are required after each country instead of commas

   b) Colons are required after each country instead of commas

   c) Semicolons are required between each city and each country

   d) No changes

4. Before long, we will be undertaking our final exams however, we have much to learn before that time.

   a) Colon after *exams*

   b) Semicolon after *exams*

   c) Remove the comma after *however*

   d) No changes

5. You have several things to accomplish before you graduate increase your keyboarding skills, develop your management skills, and obtain some experience within an office environment, to name a few.

   a) Semicolon after *graduate*

   b) Colon after *graduate* and capital letter on increase

   c) Colon after *graduate*

   d) No changes

6. The following members are part of your committee
   - Suzy Smith
   - Paul Jones
   - Samantha Rivers
     a) Semicolon after *committee*
     b) Colon after *committee*
     c) No changes

7. Note there will be a meeting tomorrow.
   a) A colon after *note*
   b) A colon after *note* and a capital letter on *there*
   c) A semicolon after *note*
   d) No changes

8. The time is 245 p.m.
   a) A colon between *2* and *4*
   b) A semicolon between *2* and *4*
   c) No changes

9. We are focusing on the following four areas family, litigation, real estate, and corporate.
   a) Colon after *areas*
   b) Semicolon after *areas*
   c) Colon after *areas* and a capital letter on *family*
   d) No changes

10. There are a couple of items we need to discuss first is your work placement and second is your career choice.
    a) Colon after *discuss*
    b) Semicolon after *discuss*
    c) Colon after *discuss* and a capital letter on *first*
    d) No changes

11. We went to Legal Aid they were presenting a seminar on the new fee schedules.
    a) Colon after *Aid*
    b) Semicolon after *Aid*
    c) No changes

12. He asked her to revise the draft agreement however, she had not yet received submissions.

   a) Colon after *agreement*

   b) Semicolon after *agreement*

   c) No changes

13. He was flying to Vancouver, British Columbia, then to Halifax, Nova Scotia.

   a) Colon after *to*

   b) Semicolon after *British Columbia*

   c) No changes

14. The statement of account was made directly following the client's appointment it was mailed out immediately.

   a) Colon after *appointment*

   b) Semicolon after *appointment*

   c) No changes

15. At 1400, we are going to meet at the courthouse.

   a) Colon after *14*

   b) Semicolon after *1400*

   c) No changes

16. Please bring the files, videotapes, and receipts for the hearing.

   a) Semicolons instead of commas after *files* and *videotapes*

   b) Colon after *bring*

   c) No changes

17. He asked for the following items

   • Files

   • Videotapes

   • Receipts

   a) Colon after *items*

   b) Semicolon after *items*

   c) No changes

18. The client made an appointment for Tuesday the appointment is to execute a will.

    a) Colon after *Tuesday*

    b) Semicolon after *Tuesday*

    c) No changes

19. You are to select one of the following Option A, Option B, or Option C.

    a) Colon after *following*

    b) Semicolon after *following*

    c) No changes

20. Note 3 Schedule of Rental Income

    a) Colon after *3*

    b) Semicolon after *3*

    c) Colon after *Note*

    d) No changes

VI. BEGINNER VOICE FILES

A. Beginner Voice File 1

Voice file: docs > CH4 > ch4beg1.mp3

Word template: docs > templates > letter.doc

Instructions: This is a letter. Use the letter template above or a template provided by your professor.

B. Beginner Voice File 2

Voice file: docs > CH4 > ch4beg2.mp3

Word template: docs > templates > letter.doc

Instructions: This is a letter. Use the letter template above or a template provided by your professor.

C. Beginner Voice File 3

Voice file: docs > CH4 > ch4beg3.mp3

Word template: docs > templates > letter.doc

Instructions: This is a letter. Use the letter template above or a template provided by your professor.

VII. INTERMEDIATE VOICE FILES

A. Intermediate Voice File 1

Voice file: docs > CH4 > ch4int1.mp3

Word template: docs > templates > voice.doc

Instructions: This is a voice message. Use the voice message template above or a template provided by your professor.

B. Intermediate Voice File 2

Voice file: docs > CH4 > ch4int2.mp3

Word template: docs > templates > letter.doc

Instructions: This is a letter. Use the letter template above or a template provided by your professor.

C. Intermediate Voice File 3

Voice file: docs > CH4 > ch4int3.mp3

Word template: docs > templates > memo.doc

Instructions: This is an interoffice memorandum. Use the interoffice memorandum template above or a template provided by your professor.

VIII. ADVANCED VOICE FILES

A. Advanced Voice File 1

Voice file: docs > CH4 > ch4adv1.mp3

Word template: docs > templates > letter.doc

Instructions: This is a letter. Use the letter template above or a template provided by your professor.

B. Advanced Voice File 2

Voice file: docs > CH4 > ch4adv2.mp3

Word template: docs > templates > letter.doc

Instructions: This is a letter. Use the letter template above or a template provided by your professor.

C. Advanced Voice File 3

Voice file: docs > CH4 > ch4adv3.mp3

Word template: docs > templates > memo.doc

Instructions: This is an interoffice memorandum. Use the interoffice memorandum template above or a template provided by your professor.

CHAPTER 5

Real Estate

I. INTRODUCTION

In this chapter, we will focus on transcription tasks that arise in the various types of real estate transactions common to many firms practising real estate.

A. Common Transactions

The majority of transactions carried out in such firms are residential purchase transactions, residential sale transactions, and residential mortgage transactions.

1. In a **purchase** transaction, the client is the **purchaser** - one or more individuals who are buying a home. The home may be a **condominium** or a **freehold** dwelling. It may be a **single family home**, **duplex**, **semi-detached home**, **row house**, or **multi-unit dwelling**. The subject land may also be **vacant land** where no home has yet been built.

   The client will be purchasing either a **resale home** or a **new home construction**. If he or she is purchasing a resale home, the **vendor** (or seller) will be one or more individuals who own the home and are selling it to the purchaser. If the client is buying a new home construction, the vendor will be a company that builds new homes.

2. In a **sale** transaction, the client is the individual or individuals who are selling a home.

3. In a **mortgage** transaction, the client is a homeowner who is arranging a new mortgage with a bank or other financial institution.

In many cases, a purchase transaction will also include a mortgage. In these cases, the purchaser is represented in both the purchase of the home and in the arrangement of the mortgage. The mortgage company may also be represented, in which case the purchaser must sign a **consent** that acknowledges a potential conflict of interest resulting from the fact that the law firm is acting for both parties.

B. Parties

The parties in a real estate transaction are:

1. the purchaser or purchasers

2. the vendor

3. the spouse of the vendor

If the spouse of the vendor is not an owner of the **property**, he or she must sign the agreement of purchase and sale (see below) and consent to the transaction.

The parties in a mortgage transaction may include:

1. the **mortgagor**, who borrows money from a bank, a private individual, or other financial institution;

2. the **mortgagee**, who lends money to a property owner; and

3. the **guarantor**, who guarantees that the mortgagor will make all mortgage payments to the mortgagee.

C. Agreement of Purchase and Sale

When a property is sold, a real estate agent or lawyer prepares a document on behalf of the purchaser that sets out the terms and conditions under which the property will be sold, called an **agreement of purchase and sale**. The agreement includes details such as:

1. the **sale price** (the price being paid by the purchaser to the vendor)

2. the **deposit** (a percentage of the sale price given by the purchaser to the vendor as a sign of good faith that the transaction will be completed)

3. **chattels** included (such as fridge, stove, washer, and/or dryer)

4. **fixtures** excluded (such as a light fixture that is a family heirloom or a stained glass window)

5. **rental items** (such as hot water tank)

6. **closing date** (the date on which the purchaser will become the new owner of the property)

7. **requisition date** (the date by which the purchaser's lawyer must send a **requisition letter** to the vendor's lawyer, detailing any problems that have been identified and that must be fixed before closing)

8. **conditions** (which must be met for the agreement to become a firm and binding contract; for example, the purchaser obtaining suitable financing, the vendor providing the purchaser with a survey of the property, or the purchaser having an inspection of the property completed)

Once it has been signed by the purchaser, the agreement of purchase and sale is given to the vendor. The vendor reviews the agreement, makes any necessary changes, signs it, and returns it to the purchaser. If the purchaser agrees to the changes, he or she signs it, and the agreement is finalized. When the conditions set out in it are met, the agreement becomes a firm and binding contract between the parties.

D. Documentation

A significant amount of documentation is required in the following stages. First, the lawyer for the purchaser orders a **title search**. This reveals all of the issues that may affect the property, such as mortgages, liens, restrictions, subdivision agreements, executions, and easements. The lawyer for the purchaser prepares a requisition letter, which outlines any issues that must be resolved before closing (such as discharges of prior mortgages and compliance with municipal planning requirements), and sends it to the vendor's lawyer before the requisition date.

The purchaser's lawyer then sends a number of **inquiry letters** to various municipal and utility departments requesting information on the status of the property and its various accounts. This is to ensure that there are no outstanding sums owing to municipalities or utilities. The number of inquiry letters sent depends on whether or not the purchaser will be obtaining **title insurance**, which can protect purchasers from defects in a property that would have been discovered had an inquiry letter been sent. Title insurance can also protect against some defects discovered in the title search.

The purchaser's lawyer prepares other documentation, which may include:

1. **direction re: title** to be signed by the purchaser, which sets out the purchaser's full name and date of birth and how they wish to take title to the property;

2. **title insurance direction** to be signed by the purchaser, which directs the purchaser's lawyer to obtain title insurance on his or her behalf;

3. **undertakings** to be signed by the vendor, where the vendor promises to do such things as leave the property vacant, fill the oil tank on closing, and pay all utility accounts to the date of closing;

4. undertaking to be signed by the vendor's lawyer, where the lawyer promises to discharge all mortgages as soon as possible following closing;

5. undertaking to re-adjust all items on the statement of adjustments, if necessary, to be signed by the purchaser (see below); and

6. **statutory declarations** to be signed by the vendor, where the vendor declares certain facts regarding the property, such as the fact that all buildings on the property are situated within the boundaries of the property.

The vendor's lawyer prepares documentation as well, which may include:

1. **transfer** from vendor to purchaser to be signed by the vendor (if paper registration) or by both parties' solicitors (if electronic registration);

2. **statement of adjustments** setting out the various monetary credits and debits to each party, resulting in the balance due on closing; and

3. **payment direction** to be signed by the vendor, which directs the purchaser's lawyer how to distribute the funds from the purchase of the home.

In a mortgage transaction, the following documents are prepared:

1. mortgage,

2. acknowledgment of standard charge terms,

3. payment direction,

4. consent acknowledging potential conflict of interest, and

5. any other documents required by the mortgagee.

E. Funds Calculations

Once the vendor's lawyer has prepared the statement of adjustments, it is given to the purchaser's lawyer and becomes the starting point for both parties to calculate their funds.

The purchaser's lawyer uses the statement of adjustments to calculate how much money the purchaser must provide in order to purchase the home, while the vendor's lawyer uses it to calculate how much money the vendor will receive on closing.

F. Glossary Term Definitions

agreement of purchase and sale	agreement between purchaser and vendor setting out terms under which the purchaser will become the owner of the property
chattels	items that will remain in the property when the purchaser becomes the owner
closing date	the date on which the purchaser will become the owner of the property
conditions	items in the agreement of purchase and sale for the benefit of either the vendor or the purchaser, which must be met in order for the agreement to become a firm and binding contract
condominium	unit where the owner owns the unit only and is part owner in the exterior of the building and the common elements
consent	document signed by a party to a transaction acknowledging a potential conflict of interest as a result of the fact that the lawyer is acting for both sides
deposit	amount of money paid by the purchaser to the vendor to show "good faith" that they will complete the transaction
direction re: title	document signed by purchaser detailing how the purchaser wishes to take title to the property such as joint tenancy or tenants in common
duplex	a house divided into two apartments
fixtures	items that are fixed to the property
freehold	a dwelling that is owned solely by the individual who purchases a property
guarantor	an individual or company that guarantees mortgage payments to the mortgagee in the event that the mortgagor defaults on mortgage payments
inquiry letters	letters sent by the law firm representing a purchaser to various utility and municipal departments requesting information on the status of the account of the current property owner
mortgage	document (also known as a "charge") registered against a property to secure the loan of monies from a financial institution to a property owner
mortgagee	financial institution that lends money to property owners and secures the loan by registration of a mortgage
mortgagor	property owner who borrows money from a financial institution
multi-unit dwelling	three or more dwelling units in one building where the units are on multiple levels of the building
new home construction	new home constructed by a builder
payment direction	direction signed by the vendor(s) in a transaction detailing how the balance due on closing is to be paid

property	land that may or may not include one or more dwelling units that is the subject of a purchase, sale, or mortgage transaction
purchase	the act of an individual or a company buying a property from another individual or company
purchaser	person or company buying a property from another person or company
rental items	items that the vendor currently rents and that the purchaser will continue to rent following closing
requisition date	the date by which the purchaser's lawyer must have reviewed the title search and submitted the requisition letter to the vendor's lawyer
requisition letter	correspondence sent from the purchaser's lawyer to the vendor's lawyer detailing any problems uncovered by the title search, building location survey, inquiry letters, or agreement of purchase and sale that need to be corrected prior to closing
resale home	a home that was owned by several companies or individuals prior to being sold to a purchaser
row house	three or more dwelling units side by side in one building
sale	the transfer of ownership of a home or property from one person or company to another person or company in exchange for financial compensation
sale price	amount of money to be paid by the purchaser to the vendor for the purchase of a property
semi-detached home	two dwelling units side by side in one building
single family home	single home on a piece of land
statement of adjustments	document setting out the financial details of the property resulting in a balance due on closing
statutory declarations	documents sworn or declared by either purchasers or vendors that contain true statements necessary to complete a real estate transaction
title insurance	policy purchased by purchasers and mortgagees protecting them from certain unknown problems affecting a property
title insurance direction	document signed by purchaser directing lawyer to purchase a title insurance policy
title search	compilation of documents prepared by a title searcher detailing all documents affecting a certain property
transfer	document that transfers ownership from one party to another
undertaking	document signed by a party promising to complete a task within a certain time frame
vacant land	land where no dwelling unit exists
vendor	person or company selling a property to another person or company

II. TERMINOLOGY EXERCISE

A. Match the terms in Column A with the definitions in Column B.

Column A		Column B
1. Condominium		a. Land that may or may not include one or more dwelling units that is the subject of a purchase, sale, or mortgage transaction
2. Single Family Home		b. Two dwelling units in one building where one unit is on each floor of the building
3. New Home Construction		c. Three or more dwelling units side by side in one building
4. Multi-unit Dwelling		d. Single home on a piece of land
5. Row Housing		e. Land where no dwelling unit exists
6. Duplex		f. Three or more dwelling units in one building where units are on multiple levels of the building
7. Semi-detached Home		g. A home that was owned by several companies or individuals prior to being sold to a purchaser
8. Resale Home		h. Unit where the owner owns the unit only and is part owner in the exterior of the building and the common elements
9. Vacant Land		i. New home constructed by a builder
10. Property		j. Two dwelling units side by side in one building

B. Match the terms in Column A with the definitions in Column B.

Column A		Column B
1. Sale Price		a. Items in the agreement of purchase and sale for the benefit of either the vendor or the purchaser, which must be met in order for the agreement to become a firm and binding contract
2. Deposit		b. Document setting out the financial details of the property resulting in a balance due on closing
3. Conditions		c. Items that are fixed to the property
4. Agreement of Purchase and Sale		d. Items that the vendor currently rents and that the purchaser will continue to rent following closing
5. Statement of Adjustments		e. The date on which the purchaser will become the owner of the property
6. Chattels		f. Amount of money to be paid by the purchaser to the vendor for the purchase of a property
7. Fixtures		g. The date by which the purchaser's lawyer must have reviewed the title search and submitted the requisition letter to the vendor's lawyer
8. Rental Items		h. Amount of money paid by the purchaser to the vendor to show "good faith" that they will complete the transaction
9. Closing Date		i. Items that will remain in the property when the purchaser becomes the owner
10. Requisition Date		j. Agreement between purchaser and vendor setting out terms under which the purchaser will become the owner of the property

III. CITATION EXERCISES

A. Rewrite each of the following by putting the units in the correct order with the correct punctuation:

1. *Livingstone v Toronto Wine Mfg Co Ltd*
    [1932] (volume)
    SCR
    175 (page)

    _____

2. [1964] (volume)
    SCR
    657 (page)
    Fraser v Minister of National Revenue

    _____

3. 3 (volume)
    CTC
    337 (page)
    Canada v Huang and Danczkay Ltd
    [1998]
    (FC)

    _____

4. *Real Estate and Business Brokers Act*
    RSO 1990
    c R.4

    _____

5. Real Estate Agents' Licensing Regulations
    YCO
    1977 (year)
    158 (regulation number)

    _____

6. 2002 ABQB 69
    Toronto Dominion Bank v Real Estate Council of Alberta
    316 (volume)
    AR
    280 (page)
    [2002]
    6 (volume)
    WWR
    276 (page)

    1 (volume)
    Alta LR
    (4th)
    154 (page)

    _____

7. (1997)
    36 (volume)
    OR
    (3d)
    462 (page)
    De Rubeis, Chetcuti v Law Society of Upper Canada
    (SC)

    _____

8. *Compar Services Inc v Foss* (1983)
    49 (volume)
    BCLR
    (SC)
    364 (page)

    _____

9. RSNB 1973
    Real Estate Agents Act
    c R-1

    _____

10. *Real Estate Trading Act*
    c R-2
    RSNL 1990

    _____

B. Rewrite each of the following citations by fixing all errors in formatting, spacing, and punctuation.

1. Real Estate Services Act S.B.C. 2004 c. 42.

_____

2. Camacho v. Dorey 2005 ABPC 373, 394 A.R. 297.

_____

3. *Manitoba Real Estate Association v. Manitoba Securities Commission*, (1999) 139 Man. Reports (2nd) 227 (Q.B.)

_____

4. Real Estate Appraisers Act S.N.S. 1998 c. 25.

_____

5. London Loan & Savings Co. of Canada v. Meagher 1930 SCR 378.

_____

6. Nova Scotia Real Estate Commission v. Lorway, 2006 NSSC 76, 241 NSR (2d) 374.

_____

7. *Real Estate Act* S.S. 1995 c. R-1.3.

_____

8. Real Estate Trading Act R.S.P.E.I. 1988 c. R-2.

_____

9. *R v Blackbird* (2005) 74 OR (3d) 241; 248 DLR (4th) 201; 192 CCC (3rd) 453.

_____

10. *Real Estate Agents' Licensing Act*, RSNWT 1988, c. 48 (Supp.).

_____

IV. GRAMMAR RULES: PLURALS AND POSSESSIVES

When a noun or a pronoun is possessive, it shows ownership of or a type of relationship to something else:

> lawyer's files (singular)

When a noun or a pronoun is plural, there is more than one person, place, or thing:

> three lawyers' files (plural)

The following are five basic rules for dealing with possessive nouns.

A. Singular Nouns

For singular or plural nouns that do not end in an "s," add an apostrophe and an "s" to the word:

> Jim's office or Evelyn's dress
>
> children's toys or men's shoes

B. Plural Nouns

For nouns that end in an "s," add only an apostrophe. There is no need to add an additional s:

> lawyers' offices
>
> companies' staff members
>
> dogs' bones

C. Hyphenated and Compound Nouns

For hyphenated and compound nouns, add an apostrophe and an "s" to the end of a hyphenated word or to the last word in a compound noun:

> My father-in-law's court case will be heard on Friday.
>
> Canada Post Corporation's website is down.

D. Two Nouns

Where two people, places, or things share ownership of something, add an apostrophe and an "s" to the second noun only:

> Jane and John's house is on Sixth Avenue.

E. Two Nouns Where Ownership Is Separate

Where two people, places, or things own things separately, add an apostrophe and an "s" to both nouns:

Jim's and Stan's cars are both blue.

If you are not sure whether a word is a possessive or a plural, the following rule will work in most cases. When you see a word that ends with an "s", look at the word immediately following it. If that word is a noun, the word with the "s" is a possessive. If it is verb, the word is a plural:

The lawyer's files are in the cabinet (noun; possessive).

The files are in the cabinet (verb; plural).

V. GRAMMAR EXERCISE: PLURALS AND POSSESSIVES

Are the following sentences correct? Answer "true" if the sentence is correct and "false" if the sentence is incorrect.

1. ____ When you graduate, you will be qualified for the legal assistants job at the courthouse.

2. ____ Welcome to the childrens' centre.

3. ____ There are four bills of lading.

4. ____ Welcome to Susan and Melissa's office.

5. ____ Please submit two months time dockets for July and August.

6. ____ The computer belongs to it's owner.

7. ____ He believes that he should be there for the distribution of his wife's estate.

8. ____ The memos enclosures were not attached.

9. ____ We need your employer's approval to open the file.

10. ____ We will prepare each others client list.

11. ____ She had to sign five account's before she could leave for the day.

12. ____ Did you invite all the MP's to the event?

13. ____ The dos and don'ts are obvious, don't you think?

14. ____ We have to dot all our i's.

15. ____ Is your bosses new wife coming to the party?

16. ____ Fifteen of our clients' want to see their portfolios.

17. ____ Can you do anyone else's job?

18. ____ My son-in-laws' parents are buying a new home.

19. ____ The Smith's asked us to handle their sale transaction.

20. ____ There are two major boards of education in our area.

VI. BEGINNER VOICE FILES

A. Beginner Voice File 1

Voice file: docs > CH5 > ch5beg1.mp3

Word template: docs > templates > memo.doc

Instructions: This is an interoffice memorandum. Use the interoffice memorandum template above or a template provided by your professor.

B. Beginner Voice File 2

Voice file: docs > CH5 > ch5beg2.mp3

Word template: docs > templates > letter.doc

Instructions: This is a letter. Use the letter template above or a template provided by your professor.

C. Beginner Voice File 3

Voice file: docs > CH5 > ch5beg3.mp3

Word template: docs > templates > voice.doc

Instructions: This is a voice message. Use the voice message template above or a template provided by your professor.

VII. INTERMEDIATE VOICE FILES

A. Intermediate Voice File 1

Voice file: docs > CH5 > ch5int1.mp3

Word template: docs > templates > memo.doc

Instructions: This is an interoffice memorandum. Use the interoffice memorandum template above or a template provided by your professor.

B. Intermediate Voice File 2

Voice file: docs > CH5 > ch5int2.mp3

Word template: docs > templates > memo.doc

Instructions: This is an interoffice memorandum. Use the interoffice memorandum template above or a template provided by your professor.

C. Intermediate Voice File 3

Voice file: docs > CH5 > ch5int3.mp3

Word template: docs > templates > letter.doc

Instructions: This is a letter. Use the letter template above or a template provided by your professor.

VIII. ADVANCED VOICE FILES

A. Advanced Voice File 1

Voice file: docs > CH5 > ch5adv1.mp3

Word template: docs > templates > memo.doc

Instructions: This is an interoffice memorandum. Use the interoffice memorandum template above or a template provided by your professor.

B. Advanced Voice File 2

Voice file: docs > CH5 > ch5adv2.mp3

Word template: docs > templates > undertaking.doc

Instructions: This is an undertaking. Use the undertaking template above or a template provided by your professor.

C. Advanced Voice File 3

Voice file: docs > CH5 > ch5adv3.mp3

Word template: docs > templates > account.doc

Instructions: This is a statement of account. Use the statement of account template above or a template provided by your professor.

CHAPTER 6

Corporations

I. INTRODUCTION

A. Incorporating a Company

In this chapter, we will focus on the transcription tasks within the area of corporate law. Law firms offer services to existing **corporations** as well as to individuals interested in incorporating a new company. Individuals may choose to **incorporate** a company rather than incur the **personal liability** risks associated with running the same business either under a **registered business name** or as a **partnership**.

When we assist one or more individuals in incorporating a new company, we need certain information from them. The lawyer representing the individuals will ask them the following questions:

1. Will they be incorporating a provincial or a federal corporation?

2. Will they choose a company name or incorporate a **numbered company**?

3. Who will be the **shareholders** of the company?

4. Who will be the **officers** of the company? What position will each officer hold such as president, vice-president, secretary, or treasurer?

5. Who will be the **directors** of the company?

6. What type of **shares** (such as common or preferred) will be issued for the company?

7. How many shares will each shareholder own?

8. How much **capital** will each shareholder contribute to the **start-up costs** of the company?

9. What will be the company's addresses? They will need an address for both the registered office and the records office.

Once these questions are answered, the process of incorporating the company can begin. First, search the name that the clients have chosen as their company name to see whether it is available. This is done through a **NUANS search**. A report is prepared indicating whether or not this name is available. The NUANS report must be filed along with the **articles of incorporation**, which are the rules and regulations that govern the conduct and activities of the company's officers and directors. Also file a **memorandum** that sets out the rules of conduct for the company, a **notice of offices**, and, if the company is to be incorporated federally, a **notice of directors**.

If the company is to be incorporated provincially, additional documents may be required.

The completed documents are filed, together with the applicable fee, with the registrar. This can be done either by mail or electronically.

B. Organizing the Corporation

The company, once incorporated, must have certain items prepared and ordered to be able to commence business.

1. CORPORATE MINUTE BOOK

One of the first things to do once the appropriate documents for incorporation have been filed, is order a **corporate minute book**. The minute book will contain all documents of the corporation, including, but not limited to:

   a. Articles of incorporation

   b. Government forms that have been filed

   c. Shareholders' **register**

   d. Officers' register

   e. Directors' register

   f. **Securities'** register

   g. All corporate **bylaws**

   h. All corporate **minutes**

   i. All corporate **resolutions**

2. CORPORATE SEAL

Although a **corporate seal** is no longer required to incorporate a company, many companies still order a corporate seal when they order their minute book, so that the officers of the company can **emboss** certain documents, such as resolutions and **share certificates**.

3. CORPORATE BANK ACCOUNT

The client will need to open a corporate bank account. The bank will require a copy of the articles of incorporation. Now, the client's new corporation is ready for business!

C. Glossary Term Definitions

articles of incorporation	form required by government that includes details of incorporated company
bylaws	rules adopted by a company defining its internal governance
capital	money invested by a shareholder into a company
corporate minute book	book that contains all pertinent documents of a corporation
corporate seal	device used to emboss the impression of a company name onto a document
corporation	company that has been incorporated under either provincial or federal laws
directors	individuals appointed within a corporation to direct the affairs of the company
emboss	create an impression onto a document using a seal
incorporate	prepare necessary documentation in order to register a company
memorandum	sets out rules for the conduct of an incorporated company
minutes	record of meeting of members of an incorporated company
notice of directors	document detailing the directors of an incorporated company
notice of offices	document detailing a company's registered office and records office
NUANS search	search for availability of a company name
numbered company	incorporated company with no specific name; rather, it is assigned the next number of incorporated companies, e.g., 101568 Canada Inc., Ltd., Limited, or Incorporated
officers	individuals within a corporation that hold a specific office, such as president or secretary
partnership	two or more individuals that start a business detailed through a partnership agreement instead of a corporation
personal liability	legal and financial responsibility of an individual with respect to the debts and obligations of a business
register	document within a corporate minute book containing all entries pertaining to a certain aspect of the corporation
registered business name	name under which a company will operate its business
resolutions	details of actions agreed to by either the directors or the shareholders of a corporation
securities	certificate showing ownership
share certificate	document detailing the number of shares owned by an individual or a company within a corporation
shareholder	person or company that owns shares in a corporation
shares	division of equity in a corporation
start-up costs	amount of money required to set up a corporation

II. TERMINOLOGY EXERCISE

A. **Fill in the blanks using the correct terminology found in the chapter introduction:**

Shane McDevitt has retained our law firm to

_____ a company for him. He would like his

company to have its own separate identity and liability. He and his

partner, Dan Smith, have decided not to register a specific name for their

company, but instead have chosen to register a

_____ so the company's identity is

anonymous. They want to incorporate rather than pursue a

_____ to reduce their chance of being sued

personally with their liability referred to as _____

_____. They have determined that in order to be able to afford to

start their new business, their _____ will be

$100,000, and, therefore, each of them will contribute $50,000 in

_____ for the company as their initial contribution to assets.

For their contributions, each will receive preferred and common

_____. They have advised us who the

_____ of the company will be, also known as

owners. They have also decided who will be the president and secretary-

treasurer of the company, known as the _____. Finally, they

have decided who the _____ will be, so that we may

complete the directors' register.

B. **Fill in the blanks using the correct terminology found in the chapter introduction:**

When Shane and Dan incorporated their company with us, we
performed a _____ to see if their preferred name
was available; it wasn't, so they decided to register a
_____ instead whereby they did not have a
name and were anonymous. They provided us with their company's two
required addresses so that we could prepare their
_____. We also prepared a
_____, which sets out the rules and conduct of the
company, as well as the _____,
detailing the activities of the company's directors and shareholders,
which was sent to the ministry to commence the incorporation. Because
they were incorporating a federal company, we also had to prepare a ____
_____. Then, we purchased a
_____ for them to hold all of the documents
of the company, as well as a _____, so they could
_____ their corporate bylaws and
_____, which itemize the shares owned by each
shareholder.

III. CITATION EXERCISE

A. Rewrite each of the following by putting the units in the correct order with the correct punctuation:

1. *Thomas W Buchanan and Dominion of Canada General Insurance Company, a body corporate v Superline Fuels Inc*

   (2007)

   272 (volume)

   NSR

   (2d)

   400 (page)

   (CA)

   _____

2. RSC

   1985

   Cape Breton Development Corporation Act

   c C-25

   _____

3. 1980-81-82-83

   SC

   Cooperative Energy Act

   c 108

   _____

4. *Mancuso v York Condominium Corporation No. 216,*

   (2008)

   292 (volume)

   DLR

   (4th)

   737 (page)

   (Ont SC)

   _____

5. c 49

   1985

   SC

   Canada Development Corporation Reorganization Act

   _____

6. [1998]

   3027 (page)

   Bates v The Queen

   2 (volume)

   CTC

   (TCC)

   _____

7. *Herring v Canada*

   43 (page)

   3 (volume)

   (FCA)

   CTC

   [2003]

   _____

8. SCR

   291 (page)

   Hargal Oils Ltd v Minister of National Revenue

   [1965]

   _____

9. *Babonau v The Queen*

   (TCC)

   [2000]

   2554 (page)

   3 (volume)

   CTC

   _____

10. [2004]

    (TCC)

    Spicy Sports Inc v The Queen

    5 (volume)

    CTC

    2090 (page)

    _____

B. Rewrite each of the following citations by fixing all errors in formatting, spacing, and punctuation:

1. Mackenzie Gas Project Impacts Act, SC 2006 c.4, s.208

    _____

2. Canada Mortgage and Housing Corporation Act, RSC 1985 c.C-7

    _____

3. Corporations and Labour Unions Returns Act Regulations, SOR/84-125

    _____

4. Lamont Management Ltd. v. The Queen [1999] 3 CTC 2576 (T.C.C.)

    _____

5. Yeats v. Central Mortgage & Housing Corp.1950 SCR 513

    _____

6. C.O.T.C. Pension Regulations SOR/61-472

    _____

7. Canadian Dredge & Dock Co. v. The Queen 1985 1 SCR, 662

    _____

8. Gurberg v. The Queen, 2002, 2 C.T.C. 2165 T.C.C.

    _____

9. Specialty Manufacturing Ltd. v. Canada, 1999, 3 C.T.C., 82 (FCA)

    _____

10. St. Germain v. Manitoba Public Insurance Corp., 2001 MBCA 135, 160 Man. R. (2nd) 1

    _____

11

IV. STYLE RULES: CAPITALIZATION

A. **Use the following capitalization rules in your transcriptions and other writings:**

1. Capitalize the beginning of a sentence.

2. Capitalize an expression used as a sentence:

    Why?

3. In a vertical list preceded by a colon, each item displayed in a list starts with a capital.

4. Capitalize after a colon if what follows can stand alone as a complete sentence; otherwise, do not capitalize.

5. Subtitles - Capitalize *all* words with four or more letters; also capitalize *most* words with fewer than four letters except the following articles, conjunctions, and prepositions: the, a, an, and, as, but, if, or, nor, at, by, for, in, of, off, on, out, to, and up.

6. For external correspondence, do not capitalize names of departments or titles of employees; you may choose to do so for internal correspondence.

7. Within a sentence, capitalize only those elements of hyphenated words that are proper nouns or proper adjectives:

    mid-Atlantic

8. Languages are capitalized:

    English

9. In a hyphenated title, capitalize only the proper noun:

    Mayor-elect

10. Capitalize proper nouns such as names and names of companies.

11. Capitalize directions that pertain to a region:

    Ottawa West

12. Do not capitalize seasons:

    summer

13. Capitalize the names of holidays:

    Labour Day

14. Never capitalize a title of a person after the person's name, even if followed by a comma:

    Mrs. Leslie Barbour, vice-president of Best Industries

15. Capitalize a title if preceding a name:

    President Robert Gilman

16. Capitalize a title of distinction:

    Prime Minister

17. Don't capitalize general degrees unless they are following a person's name:

    Cindy Johnston, Doctor of Sociology

    Robert Rutledge, M.D.

V. STYLE EXERCISE: CAPITALIZATION

A. **Are the following sentences correctly capitalized? Answer true if the sentence is correct or false if incorrect:**

1. ____ The Ontario superior court of justice is in session.

2. ____ today we have a hearing scheduled for 2 p.m.

3. ____ She replied, "thank you for applying for this position."

4. ____ Order the following supplies:

    Markers

    Pencils

    Letterhead

    Binders

5. ____ I had my surprise: my friends threw me a birthday party.

6. ____ Send that to Michel in our Human Resource Department.

7. ____ ABC moving is located on north fifth street.

8. ____ We would like to interview the French-speaking applicants.

9. ____ There are plans to open a satellite office west of the city.

10. ____ To see Paris in spring is one of my dreams.

11. ____ The Prime Minister asked for commitment on the mid-east conflict.

12. ____ Toronto is the capital city of the province of Ontario.

13. ____ He said, "Life is like a box of chocolates."

14. ____ Margo just received her master's degree and also has a bachelor of arts degree.

15. ____ The senior vice-president, Mike Gaugon, is here to greet the visitors.

16. ____ We asked president Robert Gilman to attend orientation.

17. ____ John moved to an apartment in north shore Vancouver.

18. ____ The memo is to be sent to our Managing Partner, Brenda Fitzgerald.

19. ____ The title of her new book is *How to Survive School Life From Here*.

20. ____ We only accept applicants who speak French and english.

VI. BEGINNER VOICE FILES

A. Beginner Voice File 1

Voice file: docs > CH6 > ch6beg1.mp3

Word template: docs > templates > letter.doc

Instructions: This is a letter. Use the letter template above or a template provided by your professor.

B. Beginner Voice File 2

Voice file: docs > CH6 > ch6beg2.mp3

Word template: docs > templates > letter.doc

Instructions: This is a letter. Use the letter template above or a template provided by your professor.

C. Beginner Voice File 3

Voice file: docs > CH6 > ch6beg3.mp3

Word template: docs > templates > voice.doc

Instructions: This is a voice message. Use the voice message template above or a template provided by your professor.

VII. INTERMEDIATE VOICE FILES

A. Intermediate Voice File 1

Voice file: docs > CH6 > ch6int1.mp3

Word template: docs > templates > voice.doc

Instructions: This is a voice message. Use the voice message template above or a template provided by your professor.

B. Intermediate Voice File 2

Voice file: docs > CH6 > ch6int2.mp3

Word template: docs > templates > voice.doc

Instructions: This is a voice message. Use the voice message template above or a template provided by your professor.

C. Intermediate Voice File 3

Voice file: docs > CH6 > ch6int3.mp3

Word template: docs > templates > letter.doc

Instructions: This is a letter. Use the letter template above or a template provided by your professor.

VIII. ADVANCED VOICE FILES

A. Advanced Voice File 1

Voice file: docs > CH6 > ch6adv1.mp3

Word template: docs > templates > letter.doc

Instructions: This is a letter. Use the letter template above or a template provided by your professor.

B. Advanced Voice File 2

Voice file: docs > CH6 > ch6adv2.mp3

Word template: docs > templates > letter.doc
docs > templates > account.doc

Instructions: This is a letter and statement of account. Use the letter and statement of account template above or a template provided by your professor.

C. Advanced Voice File 3

Voice file: docs > CH6 > ch6adv3.mp3

Word template: docs > templates > memo.doc

Instructions: This is an interoffice memorandum. Use the interoffice memorandum template above or a template provided by your professor.

CHAPTER 7

Family Law

I. INTRODUCTION

In this chapter, we will focus on the transcription tasks in the area of family law.

A. Compassion

It is important to keep in mind that this is a very emotional area of law. Many of the clients we see are devastated by the circumstances that have brought them to our offices, such as the breakdown of a marriage and the division of the home and its belongings. If there are children, the matter may become a custody battle. In the face of these devastating circumstances, it is critical that we provide exceptional service in a compassionate manner. Our goal is to assist in completing the process as efficiently as possible without adding to the stress of the situation.

B. Separation

Clients may approach us either before or after the initial **separation** has occurred. The separation may be amicable, hostile, or somewhere in between.

During the period of separation, before a **divorce** is granted, clients need us to negotiate and prepare a **separation agreement**. This document will set out the agreement between the parties on matters such as:

1. Will one of the parties live in the house or will it be sold?

2. How will the other assets be divided?

3. Who will the children live with?

4. When will the other spouse see the children?

5. Will one party pay **spousal support** to the other party?

6. Will one party pay **child support** to the other party?

7. Who will assume responsibility for the debts of the parties?

During the separation period, specific provincial and territorial laws govern the answers to the above questions. Once the parties have applied for a divorce, the federal *Divorce Act* applies.

C. Divorce

The majority of divorces in Canada occur after the parties have been separated for over one year. Separation becomes the reason for the divorce, as opposed to **adultery** or **cruelty**. During the divorce process, many documents are prepared and steps are followed leading up to the official divorce of the parties. These documents and steps may include:

1. **Application for divorce**
2. **Financial statement** of the parties
3. **Answer**
4. **Reply**
5. **Case conference**
6. **Discovery**
7. **Motion**
8. **Settlement conference**
9. **Trial**
10. **Divorce certificate**

D. Custody and Access

What is best for the child? This is the question that is most important when there are children involved in a divorce. The answer will be different for each family. The types of custody are:

1. **Shared custody**, where the children live with each parent at least 40 percent of the time
2. **Split custody**, where one or more children live with one parent most of the time and one or more children live with the other parent most of the time
3. **Sole custody**, where the children of the marriage live with one parent the majority of the time; this parent is the **custodial parent**

In sole custody situations, the non-custodial parent has regular **access** to the children at times that are agreed on.

E. Spousal Support

When a couple separates, the spouse with the higher income sometimes pays support to the spouse with the lower income to equal the burden of the separation, although this is not always the case. Many factors are taken into consideration when deciding on the amount of spousal support that will be paid. The federal **Department of Justice** developed the **spousal support advisory guidelines** to help in this regard. The guidelines, however, are not legislated and, as such, are just recommendations.

F. Child Support

The two parents are free to determine the amount of child support to be paid, provided both parties agree that the amount is fair. If the parents cannot agree on an amount to be paid, they can ask for a judge to decide. If they ask a judge to decide, the judge will determine an amount based on the **federal child support guidelines**.

G. Glossary Term Definitions

access	when the non-custodial parent spends time with the child of the marriage
adultery	ground for divorce when one spouse has had an extra-marital affair
answer	document that is filed in response to the application for divorce
application for divorce	document that is filed to initiate divorce proceedings
case conference	procedural step in divorce process dealing with issues such as scheduling and appointing a children's lawyer
child support	amount paid from one spouse to the other spouse to help pay for the expenses of the children of the marriage
cruelty	ground for divorce when one spouse was victimized by the other
custodial parent	parent with sole custody of the children of the marriage
Department of Justice	department of the federal government dealing with procedures of divorce in Canada
discovery	procedural step in divorce process where parties exchange financial and other information
divorce	dissolution of marriage
divorce certificate	document certifying that parties are divorced
federal child support guidelines	means of calculating child support based on income of parties and number of children of the marriage
financial statement	document itemizing the income and expenses of an individual
motion	court procedure allowing parties in an action to apply for a ruling on a particular issue before the final judgment is reached
reply	document filed with the court to dispute claims in the answer previously filed by the other party
separation	two parties of a marriage living separate and apart
separation agreement	document detailing the terms on which the parties of a marriage will live separate and apart

settlement conference	procedural step in divorce process that attempts to resolve the outstanding issues in a divorce, thereby eliminating the need to proceed to trial
shared custody	children of the marriage spend at least 40 percent of the time with each parent
sole custody	children of the marriage spend the majority of the time with one parent, the custodial parent
split custody	one or more children of the marriage spend the majority of the time with one parent, and one or more children of the marriage spend the majority of the time with the other parent
spousal support	spouse with the higher income pays an amount to the spouse with the lower income, in an effort to lessen the effects of divorce
spousal support advisory guidelines	means of calculating spousal support based on the income and expenses of the parties
trial	last step in a divorce action, wherein a judge decides the outstanding issues based on evidence received from the parties and other witnesses

II. TERMINOLOGY EXERCISE

A. **Fill in the blanks using the correct terminology found in the chapter introduction:**

Mark Hill has retained our services on a matrimonial file. He has been

_____ from his wife since he moved out over one year

ago and wants to apply for a _____. He and his wife have

already negotiated a _____, setting out the terms

of their separation; he currently pays _____

in the amount of $500 per month per child. The parties, however, have

agreed that since Mr. Hill and his wife earn a similar salary, he does not

need to pay _____ in order to support his wife.

The infant son of the parties lives solely with his mother, and she has

_____. This makes Mrs. Hill the

_____. Mr. Hill has _____

and visits with his son every Wednesday and every Saturday. Mr. Hill

wants to initiate the divorce process. The first document we need to

prepare is the _____. The grounds for the

divorce will be _____, as the parties have been living

separate and apart for more than one year.

B. **Fill in the blanks using the correct terminology found in the chapter introduction:**

We are now ready to begin work on Mark Hill's

_____ file so his marriage can be terminated legally.

He is no longer satisfied that his wife is the custodial parent and has

_____ of their son. He now wants to apply for

_____, so that their son will live part of the

time with his mother and part of the time with him. We need to amend

his initiating court documentation, the _____

_____, to reflect this change. Mr. Hill has provided us with details of

his income and expenses, so we can prepare a _____

_____. Once we receive Mrs. Hill's _____ and

financial statement, we can see if Mr. Hill agrees with the contents. If he

disputes her claims, we will prepare a _____. Using Mrs. Hill's

financial statement, we will compare the child support currently being

paid against the _____

provided by the government, indicating suggested amount of support. It

is possible that Mr. Hill may end up having to pay either more or less

_____. Mr. Hill is anxious to receive his

_____ from the court, which is the document legally

terminating his marriage, so he can remarry.

III. CITATION EXERCISE

A. Rewrite each of the following by putting the units in the correct order with the correct punctuation:

1. *Downton v Royal Trust Co et al*

   1973

   SCR

   437 (page)

   _____

2. 1987

   1 (volume)

   SCR

   857 (page)

   Richardson v Richardson

   _____

3. *Family Maintenance Regulations*

   NS Reg 181/80

   _____

4. *R v Ekman*

   2006 BCCA 206

   209 (volume)

   (3d)

   CCC

   121 (page)

   _____

5. *Civil Marriage Act*

   c 33

   SC

   2005

   _____

6. 1 (volume)

    SCR

    Lamb v Lamb

    [1985]

    851

    _____

7. *Canada Pension Plan*

    c C-8

    1985

    RSC

    _____

8. *Stemmler v May*

    (2007)

    43 (volume)

    RFL

    (6th)

    218 (page)

    (Ont SC)

    _____

9. *Lees v Lees*

    302 (page)

    (2000)

    (Ont SC)

    6 (volume)

    RFL

    (5th)

    _____

10. SOR/86-600

    Central Registry of Divorce Proceedings Regulations

    _____

B. **Rewrite each of the following citations by fixing all errors in formatting, spacing, and punctuation:**

1. Stevens v Stevens, (1982), 142 DLR (3d)376 (B.C. SC); 31 RFL (2d) 90.

2. Canada Pension Plan Regulations, CRC, c.385.

3. *Cameron v. Cameron* 1998, 43 R.F.L.-(4th) 304 (BCSC).

4. Duncan v. Duncan, 1999, B.C.C.A. 547, 178 DLR (4th) 760, 1 RFL (5th) 46.

5. Enhanced Survivor Annuity Regulations-SOR/2001-282.

6. *McLeod v. McLeod*, 2006 ABQB 927, 406 AR. 128, 69 A.L.R. (4th) 83.

7. Sather v. McCallum, (2006) ABCA 290, 32 R.F.L. (6th) 233.

8. *Federal Child Support Guidelines*, SOR / 97-175.

9. Bampi v. Mitschke, 2006 SKQB 392, 283 Sask. R. 63.

10. Divorce Act, RSC 1985, c.3 (2nd Supp.).

IV. STYLE RULES: NUMBERS

A. **Numbers 1 to 10 are spelled out; numbers 11 and greater are figures.**

B. **Dates:**

    1. When the day of the month comes after the month, no ordinal is used:

        September 21, 20xx

    2. When the day of the month comes before the month, an ordinal is used (e.g., rd, st, nd):

        21st day of September

        On September 12, we will be purchasing the new system.

C. **When using a listing of related items, numbers are written as figures:**

        2 hotdogs, 15 drinks, and 65 cookies

D. **Money:**

    1. Money in round amounts of a million must be partially presented in words:

        $15 million or 15 million dollars

    2. Repeat the word "million" to avoid misunderstanding:

        They had between $2 million and $3 million.

    3. For amounts under $1, use cents:

        25 cents

    4. When you do not have any cents, you do not include the zeros:

        $125

    5. Use figures to express amounts of money unless requested to use both figures and numbers, as in some legal documents.

E. **Spell out indefinite amounts:**

        They had thousands of investors.

F. **Spell out fractions unless in statistical or tabular material:**

        one-quarter

G. **Spell out the word "percent"; only use the percent sign (%) in statistical or tabular material. Use a figure before *percent*:**

        25 percent

H. **Use a space (not a hyphen) in a mixed fraction between the whole number and a fraction or use decimals:**

        3 3/4 or 3.75

I. Use figures when representing significant statistics or technical measurements:

> 5-year mortgage

J. Spell out ages in non-technical references, except if expressed in years, months, and days or in technical measurements.

K. Present height as figures with no comma as a separator:

> 5 feet 11 inches

L. Present distance measurements as figures and use metric abbreviations:

> 300 km

M. Years are as follows:

> 1950s or '50s

N. Instead of a dash between numbers to indicate a range, use the word "to":

> 2005 to 2006

O. Time:

1. a.m. or p.m.

2. If the time span is enclosed in either a.m. or p.m., use this designation only once:

> 8 to 10 a.m.

3. Do not use zeros if there are no minutes designated:

> 8 to 10 a.m.

4. Do not have redundancy:

> 8 a.m. in the morning - delete in the morning because *a.m.* is the morning

5. Use a figure before *o'clock* for informal language:

> 10 o'clock

6. For the 24-hour clock, no colon is used.

> 1530 or 15 30

P. In telephone numbers, put a space after the brackets:

> (613) 555-5555

Q. Use no. instead of #:

> File No. 0004-00005

R. For street addresses starting with numbers, use figures except for 1, which should be spelled out:

> One Maple Street and 25 Maple Street

V. STYLE EXERCISE: NUMBERS

A. Are the numbers in the following sentences expressed correctly? Answer true if the sentence is correct or false if incorrect.

1. ____ On October 24th, we will have a test.

2. ____ The financial statement was signed on the 10th day of September, 20xx.

3. ____ Their office had six computers, two scanners, and 15 employees.

4. ____ Wow! They just won $12 million dollars.

5. ____ Your appointment is at 2 o'clock in the afternoon.

6. ____ Our firm charges $.25 for each photocopy made on a client's file.

7. ____ It will cost you $19.00 to file a divorce certificate.

8. ____ Did you know that they stole two-thirds of the profit?

9. ____ They had fifty percent of the profits to reinvest for the following year.

10. ____ He lives at 1100-195 Fifth Avenue.

11. ____ We have 100s of inquiries each year regarding legal aid representation.

12. ____ They are getting a divorce after twenty-five years of marriage?

13. ____ Most of the students are in their 20s.

14. ____ Toronto is approximately 425 kilometres from Ottawa.

15. ____ Please call me at (613)224-2308.

16. ____ Most of you were raised in the 1980s.

17. ____ Please refer to Assignment #5.

18. ____ The meeting is scheduled from 8 a.m. to 11 a.m.

19. ____ Come see me at 2 p.m. tomorrow afternoon.

20. ____ The meeting will be held from 9 a.m. to 3:30 p.m.

VI. BEGINNER VOICE FILES

A. Beginner Voice File 1

Voice file: docs > CH7 > ch7beg1.mp3

Word template: docs > templates > letter.doc

Instructions: This is a letter. Use the letter template above or a template provided by your professor.

B. Beginner Voice File 2

Voice file: docs > CH7 > ch7beg2.mp3

Word template: docs > templates > letter.doc

Instructions: This is a letter. Use the letter template above or a template provided by your professor.

C. Beginner Voice File 3

Voice file: docs > CH7 > ch7beg3.mp3

Word template: docs > templates > voice.doc

Instructions: This is a voice message. Use the voice message template above or a template provided by your professor.

VII. INTERMEDIATE VOICE FILES

A. Intermediate Voice File 1

Voice file: docs > CH7 > ch7int1.mp3

Word template: docs > templates > memo.doc

Instructions: This is an interoffice memorandum. Use the interoffice memorandum template above or a template provided by your professor.

B. Intermediate Voice File 2

Voice file: docs > CH7 > ch7int2.mp3

Word template: docs > templates > voice.doc

Instructions: This is a voice message. Use the voice message template above or a template provided by your professor.

C. Intermediate Voice File 3

Voice file: docs > CH7 > ch7int3.mp3

Word template: docs > templates > letter.doc

Instructions: This is a letter. Use the letter template above or a template provided by your professor.

VIII. ADVANCED VOICE FILES

A. Advanced Voice File 1

Voice file: docs > CH7 > ch7adv1.mp3

Word template: docs > templates > letter.doc

Instructions: This is a letter. Use the letter template above or a template provided by your professor.

B. Advanced Voice File 2

Voice file: docs > CH7 > ch7adv2.mp3

Word template: docs > templates > letter.doc

                  docs > templates > account.doc

Instructions: This is a letter and statement of account. Use the letter and statement of account template above or a template provided by your professor.

C. Advanced Voice File 3

Voice file: docs > CH7 > ch7adv3.mp3

Word template: docs > templates > memo.doc

Instructions: This is an interoffice memorandum. Use the interoffice memorandum template above or a template provided by your professor.

CHAPTER 8

Civil Litigation

I. INTRODUCTION

In this chapter, we will focus on the transcription tasks in the area of civil litigation.

Civil litigation is an area of practice by law firms where the firm is representing a matter brought before it by the client who feels that some wrongdoing has occurred and wishes to seek compensation.

Litigation matters are undertaken by large, medium, and small law firms; legal departments within large corporations; and medical institutions such as hospitals.

Litigation is commonly known as the act of suing someone. A wrong committed by one party against another is also known as a **tort**. The most common form of tort is **negligence** whereby the wrongdoer's careless action caused harm to another. Other examples of torts are assault and trespass. Breach of contract is another common reason for litigation. Litigation is a dispute between two parties. **Class action suits** occur when a law firm represents many clients on the same matter, such as litigation against a tobacco manufacturer for injuries incurred by many as a result of its product.

Litigation is a court process of seeking compensation for **damages** as a result of this wrongdoing. There are two types of damages: liquidated and unliquidated. **Liquidated damages** can be determined by established standards or from documents submitted by the parties. An example would be the penalty specified in a contract if one of the parties breaches that contract or the amount owing on a promissory note. **Unliquidated damages** cannot be determined from the documents in the case and will need to be determined by a judge, such as compensation for injuries in an accident.

Each province and territory has its own court rules that set out the process of litigation. These rules are regulations for how to proceed and are set out in court rules of procedure.

There are two parties involved in a court action. The party commencing the action is called the **plaintiff**, and the party that is being sued is called the **defendant**.

Lawyers start by obtaining a **retainer** from the client. This is a legal document signed by the client hiring the law firm to act on the client's behalf in a certain matter. It is also known as the amount of cash advance a client gives a lawyer in trust to commence the matter. A **demand letter**, which attempts to solve the situation before a court matter begins, is then sent to the defendant. Should the defendant not comply or reply, then the lawyer will start the litigation process through the court system.

There are **limitation periods** built into the system. These are legal due dates by which parties have to file certain documents in order to maintain their legal rights. If the limitation period has passed, the person wronged loses the right to seek compensation.

The document that starts the litigation process is called the **statement of claim**; it outlines the plaintiff's version of the facts and laws that entitle the plaintiff to a remedy and the damages requested. It is filed with the court. The court opens a file and the statement of claim is served on the defendant advising that a court proceeding has been commenced.

The **title of proceeding**, also known as the style of cause, is a header on all court documents that outlines the parties involves. An example is *Smith v. Jones*. This translates to *Smith **versus** Jones*; that is, Smith is suing Jones. In terms of correspondence from the defendant, you will see Jones ats Smith. This translates to "Jones at the suit of Smith," which means that Jones is being sued by Smith.

All court documents have to be served. **Service** means ensuring that the opposing party receives a copy as determined by the rules. There are various methods of service, such as personal, courier, fax, email, and regular lettermail.

The defendant has the option of having a **statement of defence** prepared, outlining the defendant's position in relation to the statement of claim, and served on the plaintiff's lawyer. Should the defendant not respond within the limitation period, the defendant is said to be in default, and the court will issue a **judgment** based on the statement of claim. A judgment is a legal document outlining the final decision in the matter. The parties are bound by this decision, unless either one of them wishes to file an appeal.

Either party can opt to have a case heard by a **jury**, consisting of members of the community. The most common choice is not to have a jury and to let the presiding judge rule on the matter.

Again, the steps in litigation vary among provinces and territories; however, there are several similar stages:

1. **Pleadings** (statement of claim, statement of defence, and any replies)
2. **Discovery** (determining and examining the evidence to be used at trial)
3. **Pre-Trial Conference** (attempting to resolve the matter before trial)
4. **Trial** (court date with judge/jury)

At any point after the statement of defence is filed, either party can make an **offer to settle**, which has to be accepted by the opposing party. Only the plaintiff can **dismiss** the matter, which means the plaintiff abandons the matter.

Litigation is a very costly process, and before a decision is made to commence, evaluating both the client's chances of success and determining whether the defendant has the means for compensation must be considered.

A. Glossary Term Definitions

at the suit (ats)	being litigated against (sued)
civil litigation	legal dispute between parties
class action suit	a group of people who collectively bring a claim against a defendant
damages	compensation for injury or other losses
defendant	party to whom a claim is made against
demand letter	legal letter sent to opposing party requesting compensation in advance of litigation
discovery	process whereby evidence and documents to be used at trial are disclosed and reviewed
dismiss	plaintiff puts aside an action
judgment	decision made by judge at trial
jury	Canadian citizens brought together for trial to reach a verdict on an action
limitation periods	legally mandated time frames by which actions must be commenced
liquidated damages	those damages determined on the face of the documents between the parties or by established standards
negligence	causing harm to another through carelessness; the most common form of a tort
offer to settle	an invitation by a party to settle an action
plaintiff	the party bringing an action against another
pleadings	court documents outlining claims by both parties
pre-trial conference	process in which an attempt is made to resolve matter before trial
retainer	official hiring of a law firm for representation. Also known as the amount of money paid in trust to the firm in advance
service	delivery of legal documents to parties involved
statement of claim	originating document sent by the plaintiff outlining the relevant law and facts and the restitution sought
statement of defence	responding document to statement of claim outlining defendant's position
title of proceeding	header on court documents that outlines the parties involved
tort	a wrong or an injury suffered by a person for which another person can be held liable
trial	final court appearance before judge and/or jury following which a judgment is made
unliquidated damages	damages that are undetermined and need to be assessed by the court
versus (v.)	litigating against (suing)

II. TERMINOLOGY EXERCISE

A. **Fill in the blanks using the correct terminology found in the introduction:**

Diane Carson was on a city bus travelling home from a skating party with her daughter in February of last year. The bus picked up speed on the way down the hill toward the main bus terminal. The bus driver, William Jones, started to lose control, and the bus slid sideways down the hill until it came to a violent stop when it hit a curb. Diane went flying across the front part of the bus and injured herself severely. Her daughter had minimal injuries. Diane felt that it was because of the driver's negligence that the accident occurred, and she decided to see a lawyer to seek advice concerning a _____ matter.

Diane's lawyer had her sign a _____ outlining the terms of the legal representation. At this point, he also asked her to provide $2,000 in trust in order to start the matter.

William Jones expected Diane Carson to see a lawyer, who would commence an action against him for the tort of _____. He was certain that she would seek compensation in the form of _____ damages because he knew she had some injuries and that the amount of compensation would be unknown at this point (as opposed to _____ damages, whereby the compensation is already determined.)

If this matter is commenced as an action, William Jones will be known as the _____ on the legal documents and Diane Carson will be known as the _____.

According to the _____, Diane has two years less a day to commence a civil action against the bus driver. If she doesn't commence her action within that time, she will lose her right to do so.

As expected, William Jones received a _____ in the mail, suggesting that he pay the sum of $100,000 and that a payment schedule be submitted by a certain date, or Diane Carson would commence a civil litigation suit.

William Jones replied that he would not abide by the request. Diane Carson's lawyer filed a _____ with the court to start the proceeding and served William Jones with a copy.

B. **Answer true or false to each of the following:**

1. ___ Before commencing litigation, you should first determine if you
have enough evidence to support your claim and if the party you
are suing will ever have the assets to pay the damages should you
win.

2. ___ Breach of contract is the most common form of tort.

3. ___ Court rules are regulations, and each province and territory has its
own.

4. ___ A statement of defence is always filed in response to a statement of
claim.

5. ___ A class action suit is one law firm representing many clients on one
matter.

6. ___ Only the plaintiff can elect to have a jury.

7. ___ Only the plaintiff can dismiss a court matter.

8. ___ Only the defendant can make an offer to settle.

9. ___ The discovery stage is when evidence to be used at trial is
determined and examined.

10. ___ Service of a document is providing the opposing party with a copy
of a court document, as determined by the rules.

III. CITATION EXERCISE

A. Rewrite each of the following by putting the units in the correct order with the correct punctuation:

1. RSO 1990

    Registered Insurance Brokers Act

    c R.19

    _____

2. *R v Austin*

    [1996]

    1 (volume)

    SCR

    72 (page)

    _____

3. O Reg 184/97

    Teachers Qualifications

    _____

4. *Blackwater v Plint*

    [2005]

    3 (volume)

    SCR

    3 (page)

    2005 SCC 58

    _____

5. RRO 1990

    Historic Sites

    Reg 880

    _____

6. *R v Blanas*

   (2006)

   207 (volume)

   OAC

   226 (page)

   (CA)

   _____

7. c C-5

   Canada Evidence Act

   RSC 1985

   _____

8. *School Buses*

   Reg 612

   RRO 1990

   _____

9. RSBC 1996

   Negligence Act

   c 333

   _____

10. *Contributory Negligence Act*

    c C-27

    RSA 2000

    _____

B. **Rewrite each of the following citations by fixing all errors in formatting, spacing, and punctuation:**

1. Anderson v. Stevens [1981] 5 W.W.R. 550, 125 D.L.R. (3d) 736 (B.C. S.C.).

   _____

2. *Nice v. Doe*, 2000 ABCA 221, 266 A.R. 188, 190 D.L.R. (4th) 402, [2000] 10 W.W.R. 40, 83 Alta. L.R. (3d) 1 (C.A.).

   _____

3. Contributory Negligence Act, RSS 1978, c. C-31.

   _____

4. *Skyseeds Ltd. v. McLean's Agra Centre Ltd.*, 2000 S.K.Q.B. 384, [2001], 2 W.W.R. 393.

   _____

5. *Shell v. Barnsley et al.*, 2005 MBQB 190, 196 M.R. (2nd) 91.

   _____

6. *Fiset v. Toronto Police Services Board* (2001) 153 O.A.C. 153 (C.A.).

   _____

7. *Boisvert v. Leblanc*, 2005 NBQB 30, 283 NBR (2nd) 263.

   _____

8. Clarkson, Gordon Inc. v. United States Fire Insurance Company (1991), 102 N.S.R. (2d) 24 (C.A.).

   _____

9. Weeks v. Aviva Canada Inc., 2006 NSSC 83, 243 NSR(2d) 312.

   _____

10. *Contributory Negligence Act* R.S.N.W.T. 1988, c. C-18.

    _____

IV. PUNCTUATION RULES: DASHES, PARENTHESES, QUOTATION MARKS, AND UNDERSCORING

A. Dash

1. A dash is used to indicate a sudden change in thought and to emphasize what follows - use sparingly so it doesn't lose its effect

2. A dash replaces commas with non-essential modifiers

3. A dash can replace a semicolon or a colon

4. A dash is used to emphasize single words

B. Parentheses

1. Use parentheses to separate non-essential information from the rest of the sentence

2. Use parentheses to explain an abbreviation

3. Do not use a period before the closing parenthesis except with an abbreviation or when the parenthesis enclose a complete sentence

C. Quotation Marks

1. A comma appears before a direct quotation and quotation marks enclose a direct quotation

2. Direct quotations that contain a complete sentence start with a capital letter

3. Use quotation marks to cite articles, titles of chapters, or other parts of a complete work

4. Single quotation marks are used to enclose a quotation within a quotation

5. Punctuation in sentences is placed before the closing quotation marks

D. Underscoring

1. Use underscores to cite the titles of books, magazines, newspapers, plays, movies, musical compositions, and videos

2. Use underscores to refer to a word or letter

3. Use underscores to set off words being emphasized, defined, or used as examples

Note: Italics can be used to replace underscores.

V. PUNCTUATION EXERCISE: DASHES, PARENTHESES, QUOTATION MARKS, AND UNDERSCORING

A. Choose which sentence is the best use of a dash, parenthesis, quotation marks, or underscoring:

1. a) The best way (perhaps the only way) is to work overtime the next two weeks.

   b) The best way - perhaps the only way - is to work overtime the next two weeks.

2. a) Successful organizations have a common source of power (people).

   b) Successful organizations have a common source of power - people.

3. a) An immediate 10 percent salary increase will be given to any person with a CPS (Certified Professional Secretary) rating.

   b) An immediate 10 percent salary increase will be given to any person with a CPS - Certified Professional Secretary - rating.

4. a) William Smith receives a good income (he clears more than $70,000 a year as a financial planner).

   b) William Smith receives a good income - he clears more than $70,000 a year as a financial planner.

5. a) Please use the side entrance (the one on First Avenue).

   b) Please use the side entrance - the one on First Avenue.

6. a) Facsimile systems were discussed in the article <u>Facsimile Evergreening</u>, which appeared in the May issue of <u>Tech Systems</u>.

   b) Facsimile systems were discussed in the article "Facsimile Evergreening," which appeared in the May issue of <u>Tech Systems</u>.

7. a) I think we should delete "the" from the sentence.

   b) I think we should delete <u>the</u> from the sentence.

8. a) For example, <u>emigration</u> should be included in the appendix with other confusing words.

   b) For example, "emigration" should be included in the appendix with other confusing words.

9. a) We rented the video "Sound of Music" and thoroughly enjoyed watching it.

   b) We rented the video <u>Sound of Music</u> and thoroughly enjoyed watching it.

10. a) Keyboarding - that is one of your main tasks.

    b) Keyboarding (that is one of your main tasks).

11. a) We stay open late on Fridays (10 p.m.).

    b) We stay open late on Fridays - 10 p.m.

12. a) Jim Moore said "I expect the attendance to be good at our next meeting."

    b) Jim Moore said, "I expect the attendance to be good at our next meeting."

13. a) All correspondence should be answered, said the manager.

    b) "All correspondence should be answered," said the manager.

14. a) Kim asked, "Is it time to leave?"

    b) Kim asked, "is it time to leave?"

15. a) In his speech to the graduating class, Dean Franklin remarked, "I believe that, as Kelly Clarkson said, 'Take a chance, make a change, and break away.'"

    b) In his speech to the graduating class, Dean Franklin remarked, "I believe that, as Kelly Clarkson said, "Take a chance, make a change, and break away."

16. a) Do you read "The Globe and Mail?"

    b) Do you read The Globe and Mail?

17. a) Please refer to my letter of last week (July 17) for further details.

    b) Please refer to my letter of last week - July 17 - for further details.

18. a) Last week you said, "I will be there by the end of the week."

    b) Last week you said "I will be there by the end of the week."

19. a) Sally Dawson received her LLB (*Legum Baccalaureus*).

    b) Sally Dawson received her LLB - *Legum Baccalaureus*.

20. a) Please remove "spouse" from all the paragraphs and replace it with "Cindy Laplante".

    b) Please remove spouse from all the paragraphs and replace it with Cindy Laplante.

VI. BEGINNER VOICE FILES

A. Beginner Voice File 1

Voice file: docs > CH8 > ch8beg1.mp3

Word template: docs > templates > letter.doc

Instructions: This is a letter. Use the letter template above or a template provided by your professor.

B. Beginner Voice File 2

Voice file: docs > CH8 > ch8beg2.mp3

Word template: docs > templates > letter.doc

Instructions: This is a letter. Use the letter template above or a template provided by your professor.

C. Beginner Voice File 3

Voice file: docs > CH8 > ch8beg3.mp3

Word template: docs > templates > letter.doc

Instructions: This is a letter. Use the letter template above or a template provided by your professor.

VII. INTERMEDIATE VOICE FILES

A. Intermediate Voice File 1

Voice file: docs > CH8 > ch8int1.mp3

Word template: docs > templates > voice.doc

Instructions: This is a voice message. Use the voice message template above or a template provided by your professor.

B. Intermediate Voice File 2

Voice file: docs > CH8 > ch8int2.mp3

Word template: docs > templates > letter.doc

Instructions: This is a letter. Use the letter template above or a template provided by your professor.

C. Intermediate Voice File 3

Voice file: docs > CH8 > ch8int3.mp3

Word template: docs > templates > memo.doc

Instructions: This is an interoffice memorandum. Use the interoffice memorandum template above or a template provided by your professor.

VIII. ADVANCED VOICE FILES

A. Advanced Voice File 1

Voice file: docs > CH8 > ch8adv1.mp3

Word template: docs > templates > memo.doc

Instructions: This is an interoffice memorandum. Use the interoffice memorandum template above or a template provided by your professor.

B. Advanced Voice File 2

Voice file: docs > CH8 > ch8adv2.mp3

Word template: docs > templates > letter.doc

Instructions: This is a letter. Use the letter template above or a template provided by your professor.

C. Advanced Voice File 3

Voice file: docs > CH8 > ch8adv3.mp3

Word template: docs > templates > account.doc

Instructions: This is a statement of account. Use the statement of account template above or a template provided by your professor.

CHAPTER 9

Criminal Law

I. INTRODUCTION

In this chapter, we will focus on the transcription tasks in the area of criminal law. Many smaller law firms specialize in criminal representation, while large firms may include a criminal department.

In a criminal case, you will be working for **defence attorneys** who are representing clients charged with criminal offences, known as the **accused**; the individual who is wronged is known as the **victim** in a criminal case. The role of defence attorney is to ensure that every person receives a fair trial. Government lawyers called **Crown attorneys** represent the state and prosecute individuals charged with a criminal offence.

The criminal process normally begins when someone brings a complaint to a police department or the police suspect that a law has been broken. If the police have enough **evidence** to support their belief that an offence was committed, they obtain an arrest **warrant** to apprehend the person or persons they suspect committed the offence. Police have the power to detain individuals for probable cause. This is called an **arrest**.

There are two types of offences: **summary conviction offences** and **indictable offences**. Summary offences are less serious than indictable offences and include things such as trespassing and causing a disturbance. Robbery and murder are examples of indictable offences.

Following an arrest and the formal laying of charges, depending on the offence, fingerprints and photographs may be taken of the accused for police records. The accused is either kept in custody until the date set for the **bail hearing** or is released with a **summons** to appear in court. If the accused does not show up for scheduled court dates, the judge will issue a **bench warrant** authorizing the police to locate and arrest the accused.

At the bail hearing, the judge will determine whether the accused can be released. The accused may be released under his or her own word to abide by certain conditions and return for the next hearing. Or, the judge may decide that someone will have to post **bail** and take responsibility that the accused will abide by the conditions set by the judge. Alternatively, the judge may find that the accused must stay in custody until the preliminary hearing.

A date will be set for a preliminary hearing. At the hearing, the charges against the accused are read and the accused makes a **plea** of **guilty** or not guilty in answer to them. The accused must have legal representation in order to make a plea. If the accused is unrepresented by a lawyer, duty counsel at the courthouse can represent the accused **pro bono**. Following the hearing, the accused can be discharged, meaning that the accused will no longer face the charges, or will be ordered to face the charges at trial.

If the accused pleads guilty, a sentencing hearing date is set. If the accused pleads not guilty, a court date is set for a trial.

Before the trial can be held, the defence lawyers require the police to provide the details of the charges against the accused and a report indicating the evidence in the arrest of their client. This process is known as **disclosure**. Until it is complete, the defence lawyer will attend each court date and ask for an **adjournment**, whereby the trial is postponed until a later date.

Prior to a trial, the defence team must prepare a range of court documents. They also work with Crown attorneys in **judicial pre-trial conferences** to try to resolve the matter without a trial.

At **trial**, the Crown attorney presents evidence against the accused. It is not up to the accused to prove his or her innocence - he or she is innocent until proven guilty. The victim and **witnesses** also give **testimony**. The Crown will not allow **hearsay**, or testimony based upon indirect knowledge - for example, testimony as to what the witness was told by someone else. **Expert witnesses** hired by either the Crown or the defence may be called to provide credible opinion. All individuals who give testimony are bound to tell the truth.

The accused can opt for either a jury or a judge to make the **verdict**, or ruling. Most summary offences do not appear in front of a jury. For more serious offences, anyone charged with an offence that can result in more than five years imprisonment has a right to choose trial by jury. An **acquittal** is a ruling that the accused is not guilty of the charges, while a **conviction** is a ruling that the accused is guilty.

The sentence or order resulting from a conviction depends on the nature and severity of the crime and the criminal history of the accused. In general, conviction for a summary offence usually results in a fine or an order of **restitution** that requires the individual who is convicted to pay compensation for damage caused or gain made as a result of criminal activity. It may also include up to six months' imprisonment. Conviction for an indictable offence may result in a much heavier fine, **incarceration**, or both. It may also result in a conditional sentence, which is a term of sentence served in the community under supervision.

A. Glossary Term Definitions

accused	person charged with a criminal offence
acquittal	ruling that the accused is not guilty
adjournment	postponement of a trial until a later date
arrest	detainment of an individual accused of having committed a crime for probable cause

bail	surety (money or property) pledged or deposited with the court for the release of the accused with a guarantee that the accused will appear in court on the date assigned
bail hearing	hearing at which a judge determines whether an accused can be released
bench warrant	order of a judge authorizing the police to locate and arrest an accused for failing to appear in court
conviction	ruling that an accused is guilty
Crown attorney	Crown lawyer who represents the victim
defence attorney	lawyer who represents the accused
disclosure	process required before a trial in which the police provide the defence attorney with a summary of the charges and the evidence against the accused
evidence	facts, which may or may not be in dispute, pertaining to a case
expert witness	witness hired for his or her specific knowledge, skill, or experience in a particular field
guilty	plea in which an accused admits to the charges
hearsay	indirect knowledge of an event, also called third-party knowledge
incarceration	confinement of a person convicted of an offence to a correctional facility to serve a sentence
indictable offence	serious offence that may be punishable by fines over $5,000 and sentences greater than six months
judicial pre-trial conferences	conferences in which defence and Crown attorneys attempt to resolve a matter to avoid going to trial
plea	an answer of "guilty" or "not guilty" in response to a charge
pro bono	provision of legal services free of charge
restitution	court-ordered payment of compensation for damage caused or gain made as a result of criminal activity by an individual convicted of an offence to the victim
summary conviction offence	less serious offence usually punishable by fine of up to $5,000 and/or sentence of up to six months
summons	legal document issued by a court ordering an individual to appear before the court and outlining the reasons for the appearance
testimony	formal statements made by witnesses under oath before a court
trial	hearing of a matter before a judge or before a judge and jury
verdict	ruling by a judge or a judge and jury regarding disputed issues in a trial
victim	in a criminal case, the person wronged
warrant	document issued by a judge or other official authorizing the police to make an arrest or perform other acts related to the administration of justice
witness	person who has first-hand knowledge of an alleged crime

II. TERMINOLOGY EXERCISE

A. **Fill in the blanks using the terminology found in the introduction:**

In the criminal system, if the police know of a criminal act, they may have enough _____ to obtain a _____ to have the person they believe committed the offence apprehended. If the police place a person under _____, they must tell the person why he or she is being detained.

A person may be charged either with an _____ offence or a summary conviction offence. The police then decide either to _____ the accused with a promise to appear in court or to hold the accused in custody until the _____. At this hearing, the judge will either release the accused or have someone post _____ and take responsibility for the accused until the preliminary hearing.

An accused must have legal representation for this preliminary hearing. Those who do not can receive it from duty counsel _____, which means without cost; at the hearing, the accused enters a _____ of _____ or not, which determines whether the court will schedule the matter to sentencing or trial. If an accused does not show up for the court date, the judge will issue a _____ whereby the accused will be located and put under arrest for breach.

Before the trial can occur, the defence lawyer must have _____, which is full access to the police reports. Sometimes this takes weeks to obtain. The defence lawyer will attend each court date and ask for an _____, which allows the matter to be set aside until a later date.

At trial, evidence will be presented by the _____, who is a lawyer representing the state. _____ is provided by the witnesses and the victim. The court will not allow _____ evidence to be used, meaning evidence that a witness was told by a third party.

At the end of the trial, a _____ is rendered, which is the decision of the judge or jury. The outcome is either an _____, which means the accused has been found not guilty and is cleared of the charge or charges, or a _____, whereby the accused is found guilty. One penalty for serious offences is _____, whereby a person is confined to a correctional facility to serve a sentence.

III. CITATION EXERCISE

A. Rewrite each of the following by putting the units in the correct order with the correct punctuation:

1. RSC 1985

   Criminal Code

   c C-46.

   _____

2. SOR/2000-303

   Criminal Records Regulations

   _____

3. *Criminal Notoriety Act*

   c 14

   SNS 2006

   _____

4. c C-47

   RSC 1985

   Criminal Records Act

   _____

5. *Criminal Injuries Compensation Regulations*

   NS Reg 24/94

   _____

6. *R v Westergard* (2004)

   70 OR (3d) 382

   (CA)

   24 CR (6th) 375

   185 OAC 281

   _____

7. 122 CRR (2d) 241

   R v Falkner

   188 (volume)

   2004 BCSC 986

   (3d)

   406 (page)

   CCC

   _____

8. *R v Willier*

   2007 ABCA 132

   404 AR 174

   _____

9. *R v Jackson*

   573 (page)

   [1993]

   4 (volume)

   SCR

   _____

10. *R v Nette*

    SCR

    [2001]

    2001 SCC 78

    3 (volume)

    488 (page)

    _____

B. Rewrite each of the following citations by fixing all errors in format, spacing, and punctuation:

1. Criminal Records Review Act, RSBC 1996, c. 86.

    _____

2. Criminal Notoriety Act Designation Regulation, Alta. Reg. 236/2006

    _____

3. *Criminal Enterprise Suppression Act*, SS 2005, C. C-46.1.

    _____

4. *Criminal Prosecution Expenses Act*, RSNB 2011, c 134.

    _____

5. *Youth Criminal Justice Act*, SC 2002, c. 1.

    _____

6. *R. v. Leduc* (1994), 76 OAC 73 (CA)

    _____

7. *R. v. Arkell* (1988), 43 C.C.C. (3) 402, (1988), 64 C.R. (3d) 340, (1988), 30 B.C.L.R. (2d) 179 (C.A.).

    _____

8. *R. v. Tran* 2004 ABCA 35, 346 A.R. 127

    _____

9. R. v. Twigge, [1997] 5 W.W.R. 572, (1996), 148 Sask. R. 254 (C.A.).

    _____

10. *R. v. Ross*, 2003 M.B.C.A. 70, 173 Man. R. (2nd) 284

    _____

IV. GRAMMAR RULES: SUBJECTS AND VERBS

1. A verb must agree with its subject. If the subject is singular, the verb must be singular. If the subject is plural, the verb must be plural.

    I am pleased to be providing you with examples to use.

    They are planning to work on the project later this evening.

2. If there are two subjects and they are referring to one person, the verb is singular.

    Our secretary and treasurer is Leslie Avery.

3. Either/or and neither/nor take a singular verb if the subjects are singular. If both subjects are plural, then the verb is plural. If the subject is made up of both singular and plural words, the verb agrees with the nearer part of the subject.

    Neither Nathan nor Myles is able to participate in the event.

    Neither Nathan nor his employees are able to participate in the event.

    Neither the employees nor the clients are available on that date.

    Either May or June is best for the event.

    Either Nathan or his employees are able to attend.

4. Non-essential phrases should be disregarded, and the verb agrees with the main subject.

    The key element, the skills of the employees, is to be considered.

    The invoice for the computers is to be emailed shortly.

5. If the following words appear before the subject, the verb is singular: one of, each, every, either, neither, much, one.

    One of the computers is defective.

    Each person is to be treated with the greatest respect.

    Every person is to be provided with a gift of appreciation.

    Either person is to be considered for the person.

    Neither person is to be excluded from the short list.

    Much work has to be done to be ready in time for the closing date.

    One person is to volunteer to organize the celebration.

6. If the following words appear before the subject, the verb is plural: both, few, many, others, several.

> Both members of the organizing party are to be available for questions.
>
> Few people are aware of the recent changes.
>
> Many members will be participating in the upcoming fundraiser.
>
> Others are available to assist if required.
>
> Several members have declined from attending due to illness.

7. Geographic names, organizational names, publications, and product names are normally considered by the unit as singular.

> Algonquin College is one of Ontario's community colleges.
>
> The *Ottawa Citizen* has a tremendous subscriber base.
>
> Canada is a beautiful country.

V. GRAMMAR EXERCISE: SUBJECTS AND VERBS

Fill in the blanks with the correct word.

1. Every law firm _____ become more cautious recently since a local firm was vandalized.

   a. has   b. have

2. Neither the legal assistants nor the lawyer _____ to relocate.

   a. want   b. wants

3. One of the causes for errors _____ poor proofreading.

   a. is   b. are

4. The criteria for opening new files _____ to be reviewed with new staff.

   a. has   b. have

5. There _____ been no news from the managing partner in two weeks with respect to our bonuses.

   a. has   b. have

6. Our receptionist and office assistant _____ Heather.

   a. is   b. are

7. Mr. Smith, along with his three assistants, _____ going to court today.

   a. is   b. are

8. Either of the assistants _____ willing to stay late to work on the file.

   a. is   b. are

9. Attached _____ four copies of the separation agreement.

   a. is   b. are

10. Only a small percentage of our employees _____ chosen the optional benefit plan.

    a. has   b. have

11. Cameron is only one of our employees who _____ consistently working hard.

    a. is   b. are

12. Every law clerk and legal assistant on staff _____ to work on the class action law suit.

   a. want   b. wants

13. Our survey, along with the previous study, _____ that the students are satisfied.

   a. prove   b. proves

14. Here _____ a descriptive report and a copy of the document.

   a. is   b. are

15. Berry & Asselin _____ provided many students with community service hours.

   a. has   b. have

16. Every legal assistant _____ been provided with a new computer.

   a. has   b. have

17. Both the paralegals and the legal assistants _____ to undertake training on the new software programs.

   a. is   b. are

18. None of the paralegals _____ to be reassigned at the moment to the new branch office.

   a. wish   b. wishes

19. Neither the managing partner nor the director of finance _____ to lift the hiring freeze.

   a. want   b. wants

20. The management committee _____ voting today on the new directives.

   a. is   b. are

VI. BEGINNER VOICE FILES

A. Beginner Voice File 1

Voice file: docs > CH9 > ch9beg1.mp3

Word template: docs > templates > voice.doc

Instructions: This is a voice message. Use the voice message template above or a template provided by your professor.

B. Beginner Voice File 2

Voice file: docs > CH9 > ch9beg2.mp3

Word template: docs > templates > letter.doc

Instructions: This is a letter. Use the letter template above or a template provided by your professor.

C. Beginner Voice File 3

Voice file: docs > CH9 > ch9beg3.mp3

Word template: docs > templates > letter.doc

Instructions: This is a letter. Use the letter template above or a template provided by your professor.

VII. INTERMEDIATE VOICE FILES

A. Intermediate Voice File 1

Voice file: docs > CH9 > ch9int1.mp3

Word template: docs > templates > letter.doc

Instructions: This is a letter. Use the letter template above or a template provided by your professor.

B. Intermediate Voice File 2

Voice file: docs > CH9 > ch9int2.mp3

Word template: docs > templates > letter.doc

Instructions: This is a letter. Use the letter template above or a template provided by your professor.

C. Intermediate Voice File 3

Voice file: docs > CH9 > ch9int3.mp3

Word template: docs > templates > memo.doc

Instructions: This is an interoffice memorandum. Use the interoffice memorandum template above or a template provided by your professor.

VIII. ADVANCED VOICE FILES

A. Advanced Voice File 1

Voice file: docs > CH9 > ch9adv1.mp3

Word template: docs > templates > letter.doc

Instructions: This is a letter. Use the letter template above or a template provided by your professor.

B. Advanced Voice File 2

Voice file: docs > CH9 > ch9adv2.mp3

Word template: docs > templates > memo.doc

Instructions: This is an interoffice memorandum. Use the interoffice memorandum template above or a template provided by your professor.

C. Advanced Voice File 3

Voice file: docs > CH9 > ch9adv3.mp3

Word template: docs > templates > account.doc

Instructions: This is a statement of account. Use the statement of account template above or a template provided by your professor.

CHAPTER 10
Intellectual Property

I. INTRODUCTION

In this chapter, we will focus on the transcription tasks in the area of intellectual property.

Intellectual property is a growing area of legal practice. Some law firms specialize only in this area.

Intellectual property refers to the right to control specific creations of the mind recognized by law, and it includes written material, performances, visual art, architecture, software, product designs, and practical applications of scientific principles.

Intellectual property law governs both commercial and artistic creations. This area of law operates by protecting those who create new works, allowing them to distribute their works without worrying that someone else will copy them or exploit their reputation. Copyright generally governs artistic creations; patents protect scientific applications and new technology development. Specific areas of technology have their own legislation; for instance, there is legislation that protects the development of integrated circuits, while breeders' rights legislation protects the product of breeding programs. Trade-mark and industrial design refer to the cosmetic appearance of a product. Intellectual property protection is an important part of international trade and helps keep innovation profitable.

The **Canadian Intellectual Property Office (CIPO)** is located in Gatineau, Quebec. It is a special operating agency associated with Industry Canada, and it is responsible for the administration and processing of intellectual property in Canada. CIPO's website is: www.cipo.ic.gc.ca.

Intellectual property has federal jurisdiction under the following acts, and each act has its own regulations:

- *Patent Act*
- *Trade-marks Act*
- *Copyright Act*
- *Integrated Circuit Topography Act*
- *Industrial Design Act*
- *Plant Breeders' Rights Act*

Certain types of intellectual property have their own electronic Internet federal databases for searching purposes; for example, the Canadian Patent Database and the Canadian Trade-mark Database.

A. Patents

Patents offer inventors a source of protection for their products and processes. They give inventors the exclusive right to exploit their inventions. In return for this protection, inventors make the information relating to the patented invention public, creating a repository of useful technical information for the public, allowing further technological development to take place. Patents can be issued for improvements to existing inventions.

In order for CIPO to approve a patent, an examiner looks for novelty (newness), utility (usefulness), and inventiveness/ingenuity (uniqueness).

A patent may be obtained for the product itself, for some aspect of the product, or for an apparatus to make the product.

A patent must be registered in each country if the inventor wishes to receive protection in that country. Registering with the European Union guarantees the registration within 27 countries. Protection lasts 20 years from date of filing, and it is not renewable.

Sometimes there is a label affixed to new products as patent pending. This informs others that the inventor has applied for a patent and that legal protection from **infringement** (including retroactive rights) may be forthcoming.

It is important to keep a patent secret until an **application** is filed with CIPO. A patent must be filed within one year of its creation.

B. Trade-marks

Trade-marks are words, symbols, pictures, logos, designs, sounds, smells, shape of goods, or a combination of these elements that distinguish certain goods or services of one person or organization from those of others in the marketplace. Trade-marks allow their owners exclusive use of that mark to be identified with their goods or services. The protection lasts 15 years, and it is renewable indefinitely every 15 years.

A **trade name** is the name under which a business is conducted and can be registered as a trade-mark. To do so, it must be identifiable by the product or service being provided; for example, Coke and Coca-Cola (both are registered trade-marks).

C. Industrial Designs

An **industrial design** is any original shape, pattern, or ornamentation applied to a useful article that is mass-produced. It may be made by hand, tool, or machine.

An industrial design is the visually appealing part of the design; for example, the shape of a table or the decoration on a plate, and it can be protected for ten years from the date of registration. Maintenance of the registration of a design is subject to payment of a maintenance fee during the first five years.

D. Copyright

Copyright is a property right that allows only the creator—or someone under contract with the creator—the right to publish or copy an original literary, dramatic, musical, or artistic work. A copyright is automatically acquired by the creator when an original work is created. The copyright is protected by the law on proof of authorship; therefore, there is no need to file for protection. However, there is a registration process that will help protect the copyright if it is challenged.

Permission must be obtained from the author to use his or her work, and the term of protection is for life plus 50 years after the death of the author.

The recognizable commercial symbol for registered copyright is ©.

Royalties are sums paid to copyright, patent, and trade-marks owners for the sale or use of their works. A contract must be signed first in order to receive royalties.

Plagiarism occurs when the work, or part of it, is used by another person who claims it as his or her own and does not have the permission of the author.

E. Integrated Circuit Topographies

Integrated circuit topographies are three-dimensional configurations of the electronic circuits used in microchips and semiconductor chips. Exclusive ownership rights are for ten years on the original circuit design; protection can extend to the layout design as well as to the finished product.

F. Plant Breeders' Rights

Plant breeders' rights provide rights to new varieties of some plant species. Varieties must be new (not previously sold), different from all other varieties, uniform (all plants are the same), and stable (each generation is the same).

A description must be submitted to the *Plant Varieties Journal*. If the claim is granted, the plant breeder is entitled to control the multiplication and sale of the seeds for up to 18 years, but other people are allowed to breed, save, or grow the protected varieties for their own private use.

Protection is available through the **International Union for the Protection of New Varieties of Plants (UPOV)** who provides and promotes an effective system of plant variety protection with the aim of encouraging the development of new varieties of plants.

Each intellectual property area process is different; however, there are some commonalities between them in the steps. It is important that intellectual property is protected by having a **non-disclosure** agreement signed by anyone interested in seeing or hearing about the idea. This protects the creator from having it stolen. The intellectual property **agent** will sign one as well.

G. Trade-mark Process

The following stages occur when obtaining approval for a trade-mark, which is similar to other areas of intellectual property:

- Availability **searches** involve checking databases to see if the intellectual property already exists

- **Filing** is the first stage with CIPO whereby the intellectual property application is filed. A **declaration** is signed stating that the creator is entitled to the trade-mark. A receipt of filing is provided from CIPO.

- **Examination** occurs when the **examiner** from CIPO reviews the application and provides a report of areas of concern, if any.

- **Approval** occurs when the application is approved by the examiner and a notice of approval is sent.

- **Advertisement** occurs when the application is **advertised** in a journal, such as the *Trade-mark Journal* for a trade-mark application.

- **Opposition** occurs when a claim is made against an application; it is a challenge to the application.

- **Allowance** occurs when there is no opposition to the **application**. A notice of allowance is issued indicating that the application is ready for registration.

- **Registration** is the final stage in the process whereby the application has been approved and is **registered**. A certificate of registration is issued.

Infringement can occur if the rights of the intellectual property owner are violated. It is up to the owner or the owner's representative to police the intellectual property to ensure that it is not being infringed.

Abandonment occurs when the applicant decides not to proceed with an application, perhaps due to its rejection.

H. Glossary Term Definitions

abandonment	application is not registered
advertised	application is made public knowledge
advertisement	application is advertised in journal
agent	individual working for an intellectual property company who assists in getting application approved through CIPO
allowance	if there is no opposition to application, application is approved and is ready for registration
application	initial submission to CIPO in the process of receiving intellectual property right
approval	application is approved by CIPO

CIPO	Canadian Intellectual Property Office, responsible for administering and processing intellectual property
copyright	protection of expression and exclusive right to an author's original work
declaration	sworn statement of entitlement to intellectual property, which is part of application
examination	application is reviewed in detail
examiner	CIPO employee who reviews application and writes a report based on the findings of the examination
filing	application is made to CIPO
industrial design	protection of the original shape, pattern, or ornamentation of an article that is mass-produced
infringement	owner's Intellectual property rights are violated
integrated circuit topographies	protected three-dimensional configurations of the electronic circuits used in microchips and semiconductor chips
intellectual property	exclusive rights over creations of the mind
non-disclosure agreement	binding document signed between two parties whereby ideas discussed will be kept confidential
opposition	occurs when a claim is made against application
patent	protected invention that is new, useful, and unique in terms of its mechanism or operation
plagiarism	claiming someone else's work a your own without permission of the author
plant breeders' rights	protected rights to new varieties of certain plant species
registered	application receives approval by CIPO
registration	final approval of application and application is registered
royalties	percentage of revenue paid to intellectual property owners for sale or use of their work
searches	determining if intellectual property already exists
trade-mark	protected distinctive identity of a product, such as its words, symbols, logo, pictures, and designs
trade name	business name
UPOV	International Union for the Protection of New Varieties of Plants, responsible for plant breeders' rights

II. TERMINOLOGY EXERCISE

A. Answer true or false to each of the following:

1. ____ CIPO stands for the Canadian Intellectual Property Organization.

2. ____ CIPO is affiliated with Industry Canada and is responsible for administering and processing intellectual property.

3. ____ Intellectual property protects an original idea.

4. ____ Intellectual property spans the following areas when protecting creative endeavours: trade-marks, patents, industrial designs, copyright, integrated circuit topographies, and plant breeders' rights.

5. ____ Trade-marks can be designs and words and must be renewed every ten years.

6. ____ Patents are government grants that give inventors exclusive rights to their inventions; this right is only valid for 15 years after an application has been filed, and they can only be filed in Canada.

7. ____ A patent is granted for items that are new, useful, and obvious, and only for ideas, not processes.

8. ____ Industrial designs deal with the shape, pattern, or ornamentation of an item.

9. ____ Copyright applies to all original works, including music, and it is the protection, for the author's life plus 50 years, of expression, and it is the exclusive right for the owner to one's material whereby an application does not have to be filed in order to be protected.

10. ____ Integrated circuit topographies protect the three-dimensional configuration of electronic circuits used in micro- and semiconductor chips.

B. **Fill in the blanks using the correct terminology found in the introduction.**

You have decided you want to register a trade-mark. You need assistance
since you don't know how to do it yourself. You would contact an
_____ who would do this for you for a fee.

At this point, you will be encouraged to not discuss your trade-mark
with anyone until it has been filed. If you are planning to, you should get
a _____ document signed.

Once the preliminary searches have been done, an
_____ is filed with _____. This
document has a _____ that you must sign, stating
that you are entitled to the trade-mark. You receive a receipt of filing.

The next stage is undertaken by an _____, who
reviews the file to determine if the trade-mark meets the requirements
under the *Trade-mark Act*. If there are no problems, it is
_____ in the *Trade-mark Journal*, which is
electronically issued each Wednesday. If there is no
_____, it is _____, and a certificate is
issued.

It is up to the creator to police his or her own intellectual property.
_____ occurs when someone violates the creator's
intellectual property.

III. CITATION EXERCISE

A. Rewrite each of the following by putting the units in the correct order with the correct punctuation:

1. 3 (volume)

    2005 SCC 65

    Kirkbi AG v Ritvik Holdings Inc

    [2005]

    SCR

    302 (page)

    _____

2. *Copyright Regulations*

    SOR/97-457

    _____

3. RSC 1985

    Patent Act

    c P-4

    _____

4. (Alta QB)

    Bank of Montreal v Scaffold Connection Corp

    36 CBR (4th) 13

    2002 ABQB 706

    _____

5. Sask R

    2004 SKQB 15

    (Sask QB)

    Nadon v United Steel Workers of America

    244 (volume)

    255 (page)

    _____

6. Sask R

    Mantei v Morris

    168 (volume)

    18 (page)

    [1998]

    741 page

    WWR

    _____

7. SCR

    1132 (page)

    Duquet v Town of Sainte-Agathe

    [1977]

    2 (volume)

    _____

8. SOR/96-423

    Patent Rules

    _____

9. *Integrated Circuit Topography Act*

    c 37

    SC 1990

    _____

10. SC 1990

    Plant Breeders' Rights Act

    c 20

B. Rewrite each of the following citations by fixing all errors in formatting, spacing, and punctuation:

1. Formea Chemicals Ltd. v. Polymer Corp. Ltd., (1968) S.C.R. 754.

   ---

2. *R. v. Demers*, 2004 SCC 46 [2004] 2 S.C.R. 489

   ---

3. Trade-marks Regulations, SOR/96-195.

   ---

4. *Trade-marks Act*, RSC. 1985, c. T-13.

   ---

5. *Mortil v. International Phasor Telecom Ltd.* (1988), 20 C.P.R. (3rd) 277 (BC SC).

   ---

6. *Maple Leaf Foods Inc. v. Butler*, 2002 MBQB 82 17 C.C.E.L. (3d) 44, 23 B.L.R. (3d) 141, 162 Man. R. (2nd) 293 (Man. Q.B.).

   ---

7. *Carleton University v. Geonetix Technologies Inc./Technologies Geonetix Inc.* (2001),27 C.B.R. (4th) 20 (ON SC).

   ---

8. *MacLellan v. MacLellan* 2001 NBCA 82, 18 RFL (5th) 322 (N.B. C.A.)

   ---

9. *Robert D. Sutherland Architects Ltd. v. Montykola Investments Inc.* (1995), 142 NSR (2d) 137, 61 CPR (3d) 447 (N.S. S.C.).

   ---

10. *Dhillon v. Dhillon* 2001 YKSC 543, 22 R.F.L. (5th) 269 (Yuk. S.C.).

IV. HYPHENATION RULES: COMPOUND WORDS

A. Compound nouns do not follow a regular pattern.

B. They can be written as one word, with spaces, or hyphenated.

C. If a compound noun is not listed in a dictionary, treat it as two words.

D. There are no spaces before or after the hyphen - it is not a dash.

E. Compound adjectives consist of two or more words that function as a unit and express one thought, such as:

> follow-up report

F. Compound adjectives usually require a hyphen when they are before the noun.

G. When compound adjective words occur as individual words in a sentence in the normal order, they do not require a hyphen. They are now verbs rather than adjectives.

> Please follow up on that report

H. When the prefix of a word ends with the same letter as the first letter of the root word or there are two vowels together:

> re-establish and semi-annual

V. SPELLING EXERCISE: COMPOUND WORDS

Answer true if the compound words (nouns and adjectives) are written correctly, and false if not.

1. ____ Interest rates for five-year mortgages have been holding steady.

2. ____ You are second year students.

3. ____ Please keep me up to date on the litigation seminar.

4. ____ Did you include staff training in your long-range budget costing?

5. ____ We try to maintain a state of the art lead in our technology.

6. ____ We have a firm retreat semi annually at Chateau Montebello.

7. ____ You will be finished your qualifications mid April.

8. ____ Is he looking for full time employment as a legal assistant?

9. ____ All staff will be receiving a cost-of-living increase each year in addition to the performance increase.

10. ____ Did you follow up with your mentor?

11. ____ When you fly to Amsterdam, do you want a round-trip ticket?

12. ____ Is the follow up report ready for tomorrow's meeting?

13. ____ She just completed her second year with this firm.

14. ____ Are you preparing the thank-you notes for the presenters?

15. ____ Did they attend the high level meeting last week?

16. ____ Did you re-examine the file before he went to court?

17. ____ It is a 12 hour journey to the conference.

18. ____ There is going to be a ten week delay.

19. ____ They are having a face-to-face meeting rather than a conference call.

20. ____ They are conducting the interview on a trial and error basis.

VI. BEGINNER VOICE FILES

A. Beginner Voice File 1

Voice file: docs > CH10 > ch10beg1.mp3

Word template: docs > templates > voice.doc

Instructions: This is a voice message. Use the voice message template above or a template provided by your professor.

B. Beginner Voice File 2

Voice file: docs > CH10 > ch10beg2.mp3

Word template: docs > templates > letter.doc

Instructions: This is a letter. Use the letter template above or a template provided by your professor.

C. Beginner Voice File 3

Voice file: docs > CH10 > ch10beg3.mp3

Word template: docs > templates > letter.doc

Instructions: This is a letter. Use the letter template above or a template provided by your professor.

VII. INTERMEDIATE VOICE FILES

A. Intermediate Voice File 1

Voice file: docs > CH10 > ch10int1.mp3

Word template: docs > templates > letter.doc

Instructions: This is a letter. Use the letter template above or a template provided by your professor.

B. Intermediate Voice File 2

Voice file: docs > CH10 > ch10int2.mp3

Word template: docs > templates > letter.doc

Instructions: This is a letter. Use the letter template above or a template provided by your professor.

C. Intermediate Voice File 3

Voice file: docs > CH10 > ch10int3.mp3

Word template: docs > templates > memo.doc

Instructions: This is an interoffice memorandum. Use the interoffice memorandum template above or a template provided by your professor.

VIII. ADVANCED VOICE FILES

A. Advanced Voice File 1

Voice file: docs > CH10 > ch10adv1.mp3

Word template: docs > templates > letter.doc

Instructions: This is a letter. Use the letter template above or a template provided by your professor.

B. Advanced Voice File 2

Voice file: docs > CH10 > ch10adv2.mp3

Word template: docs > templates > memo.doc

Instructions: This is an interoffice memorandum. Use the interoffice memorandum template above or a template provided by your professor.

C. Advanced Voice File 3

Voice file: docs > CH10 > ch10adv3.mp3

Word template: docs > templates > memo.doc

Instructions: This is an interoffice memorandum. Use the interoffice memorandum template above or a template provided by your professor.

CHAPTER 11

Landlord and Tenant

I. INTRODUCTION

In this chapter, we will focus on transcription tasks in the **landlord** and **tenant** area of law.

Law firms typically represent two types of landlords in this area of law. The first are those who do the majority of work with regard to their **rental properties** themselves and consult law firms only when they have problems with tenants. The second are those who retain law firms to do everything for them with respect to their rental properties.

A. Leases

Clients who purchase a rental property must first find a tenant or tenants. Next, they need to have the tenant or tenants sign a **lease**. Law firms often become involved at this stage, especially if there has been a recent change in **legislation**, if the landlord has not had a tenant before, or if the landlord has not had a tenant for some time.

A firm retained by a landlord to prepare a lease must ensure that the lease reflects the most recent provincial legislation in landlord and tenant law. The lease will set out:

1. Complete name(s) of the landlord(s) and tenant(s)

2. Address of the rental property and the specific unit that is the subject of the lease

3. **Rental period**, amount of **rent** per rental period, due date of the rent payments (such as the first day of each month), and the person to whom the rent is to be paid

4. Whether **post-dated cheques** are required

5. Amount of any **prepaid rent** due, which is often required as a security deposit

6. Whether or not the rent includes **utilities**, such as gas, water, and hydro

7. What utilities are available and who is responsible for paying for them

8. Whether any parking spaces may be used by the tenant, and if so, where they are located and whether the tenant must pay additional costs to use them

9. How the tenant is to reach the landlord in case of emergency

10. What appliances, if any, are included in the unit

11. Who is responsible for various maintenance involving the property, such as grass cutting and snow removal

12. What procedures will be followed if the tenant does not pay rent on time or if the tenant's rent cheque **bounces**

The tenant(s) and the landlord(s) will sign and date the lease. A signed and dated copy should be given to both parties. Usually, when the tenant delivers the executed lease to the landlord, the tenant also provides the landlord with **first month's rent**, **last month's rent**, and post-dated cheques for the remainder of the rental period, if required.

B. Landlord and Tenant Obligations

The lease may include **rules and regulations** that outline the obligations of the landlord and tenant with respect to various maintenance items, such as:

1. Maintenance of appliances included at the property and in the rental unit

2. General maintenance of the interior and exterior of the property

3. Painting of the rental unit at the beginning and end of the rental period

4. Maintenance of safety devices such as fire alarms and smoke detectors

5. Major exterior repairs such as roof and foundation

The rules and regulations may also contain items regarding noise, pets, and smoking on the property and in the rental unit

C. Rent Increases

Landlords may require a law firm to prepare, on their behalf, **notices of rent increase**. In drafting such notices, the firm must ensure that the increase does not exceed the increase permitted by the provincial guidelines. The firm must also ensure that the notices are properly signed, either by the landlord or by the firm as **agent** for the landlord. The notice of rent increase must be delivered within the time frame for **notice** required by the appropriate provincial or federal legislation.

D. Notices to Vacate Premises

Landlords may want a particular tenant or tenants to vacate the premises for various reasons, including:

1. Landlord requires the premises for personal use or for the use of a family member

2. Landlord needs to perform major maintenance work on the premises

3. Lease period is over and the landlord does not wish to renew the lease

4. Tenant is on a **month-to-month lease** and the landlord wants to terminate the tenancy

5. Tenant is in **default** of rental payments

6. Tenant has damaged the property

Landlords who wish to have particular tenants removed from their rental properties may retain a firm to prepare a **notice to vacate the premises**. As in the case of a notice of rent increase, the firm must ensure that the conditions are in place for an eviction to take place under the appropriate legislation; that the notice to vacate the premises is properly signed, either by the landlord or by the firm as agent for the landlord; and that it is delivered within the time frame for notice required by the appropriate provincial or federal legislation.

E. Court or Tribunal Action

A landlord or tenant who believes that the other party has not fulfilled its obligations with respect to the property may initiate a **court or tribunal action** in accordance with the provincial, territorial, or federal guidelines applicable to the particular area of residency. This will entail the preparation of documentation by a firm on behalf of the client, such as affidavits of witnesses and specific forms required by the court or tribunal. The matter will be given a date for hearing and will be heard by the court or tribunal on that day. The parties will be required to adhere to the decision of the court or tribunal.

F. Glossary Term Definitions

agent	person acting on behalf of someone, such as the owner of a property
bounce	of a cheque, to be returned by a bank when there are insufficient funds in the payor's bank account to cover the payment
court or tribunal action	proceeding between two parties where a presiding body decides a disputed action
default	fail to make payments previously agreed to
first month's rent	first monthly rental payment
landlord	owner of a rental property
last month's rent	security deposit in the amount of one month's rent that will be applied toward the tenant's final month of residence in a rental property
lease	document providing details of agreement between landlord and tenant
legislation	government-regulated rules that set out procedures in certain areas of law
month-to-month lease	agreement between landlord and tenant regarding a rental property where parties are not bound for a one-year term
notice	provision of information as required by law to make the recipient aware of a fact or thing

notice of rent increase	document sent from landlord to tenant advising that the fees for residing in the rental property will be increasing
notice to vacate the premises	document sent from landlord to tenant providing notice that the tenant must vacate the premises and providing details regarding the reasons why and the time by which the tenant must vacate
post-dated cheques	cheques given from tenant to landlord that are dated in the future and will cover upcoming rental payments
prepaid rent	rental payments that have been paid in advance of their due dates
rent	amount paid from tenant to landlord in exchange for the right to occupy the rental property
rental period	amount of time that a tenant is permitted to occupy a rental property
rental property	property that is the subject of a lease
rules and regulations	terms outlining the obligations of the parties in an agreement
tenant	person entitled to live at a rental property in exchange for payment of rent to the landlord
utilities	services to a property provided by a company supplying water, gas, and hydro

II. TERMINOLOGY EXERCISE

A. Fill in the blanks using the correct terminology found in the introduction:

Our latest client is Andrew McLean, a _____ who owns a number of houses occupied by tenants. He has just bought a new

_____ that he wants to lease out. He has found a _____ who wants to move into the property and he has already prepared his own _____, setting out the terms of the tenancy. He has received _____ from the tenant to pay for their first month of residency, as well as a security deposit in the form of _____. The tenant also gave him a series of _____ for payment of the monthly rent for the entire _____.

B. Fill in the blanks using the correct terminology found in the introduction:

An existing client of ours, Andrew McLean, has a tenant who has not paid rent for two months. His last two cheques _____, and Mr. McLean wants us to prepare a _____

_____ so that he can start the process of evicting the tenant from the property. The lease has expired, meaning the

_____ is over and the tenant is on a

_____ rather than subject to yearly lease. One of the months of unpaid rent has been covered by the deposit or _____, however, the tenant is still in _____ of his rental payments as there is still one month of unpaid rent. Mr. McLean prepared a _____ and served it on the tenant; however, the tenant has not vacated the premises. According to our provincial _____, Mr. McLean is now entitled to proceed with a _____ against the defaulting _____.

Mr. McLean also suspects that the tenant has not paid the _____, including hydro and gas, at the premises either. He just wants the _____ to be vacated.

III. CITATION EXERCISE

A. Rewrite each of the following by putting the units in the correct order with the correct punctuation:

1. *Business Practices Permissible to Landlords in Selecting Prospective Tenants for Residential Accommodation*
   O Reg
   290/98

   _____

2. SKQB
   Kusch v Kusch
   2006
   419
   287 (volume)
   Sask R
   1 (page)

   _____

3. (1994)
   Nova Developments Ltd v MacDonald
   137 (volume)
   NSR
   (2d)
   (SC)
   318 (page)

   _____

4. c 188
   Soldier Settlement Act
   RSC
   1927

   _____

5. *Mobile Home Sites Tenancies Act*
   c M-20
   RSA 2000

   _____

6. c R-22.001
    2006
    SS
    Residential Tenancies Act, 2006

---

7. 2601
    Okanagan Prime Products Inc v Henderson
    BCCA
    1996
    28 (volume)
    BCLR
    137 (page)
    (3d)

---

8. (2003)
    Zellers Inc v Orlando Corporation
    OR
    66 (volume)
    (3d)
    535 (page)
    175 (volume)
    OAC
    192 (page)
    (CA)

---

9. RSC
    1985
    Territorial Lands Act
    c T-7

---

10. *Residential Tenancy Regulation*
    477/2003
    BC Reg

B. Rewrite each of the following citations by fixing all errors in formatting, spacing, and punctuation:

1. *London Property Management v. McIndoe* (1995), 134 Man. R. (2nd) 310 (C.A.)

   _____

2. *Pinheiro v. Bowes* (1994) 109 D.L.R. (4th) 315 (Ont. S.C)

   _____

3. *Holy Spirit Credit Union v. Gurevich*, 2000 M.B.C.A. 37, 187 DLR (4th) 219, 145 Man. R. (2d) 285; [2000] 7 WWR 34.

   _____

4. Athanasiou et al. v. Palmina Puliafito Co. et al., [1964] SCR 119.

   _____

5. T. Eaton Co. v. Canada, [1999] 3 F.C.A. 123 F.C.A.; 53 DTC 5178; [1999] 2 CTC 380.

   _____

6. Bovey v. Gananoque (Town) 1992 2 S.C.R. 5.

   _____

7. National Parks Signs Regulations, CRC, c. 1130

   _____

8. Ikea Ltd. v. Canada 1998 1 SCR 196.

   _____

9. Landlord and Tenant Act, RSNB 1973, c. L-1.

   _____

10. *Residential Tenancy Regulation*, BC Reg. 477/2003.

   _____

IV. GRAMMAR RULES: PRONOUNS

A pronoun is a word that takes the place of a noun. There are four types of pronouns: subject, object, possessive, and reflexive.

A. Subject

1. Subject pronouns are used when the pronoun is the subject of the sentence. The subject of a sentence is the person or thing performing an action.

2. The subject pronouns are "I," "you," "he," "she," "it," "we," and "they."

   I sent the copies.

B. Object

1. Object pronouns are used when the pronoun is the object of a verb, a preposition, or an infinitive phrase.

2. The object pronouns are "me," "you," "him," "her," "it," "us," and "them."

   Are you talking to me?

3. To decide whether to use a subject pronoun or an object pronoun in a particular sentence, try completing the sentence in your head:

   John is taller than _____ (I/me).

   In this case, you would complete the sentence as "John is taller than I (am)," so the subject pronoun "I" is the correct choice.

4. Sometimes, using one pronoun instead of another changes the meaning of a sentence:

   Susan would rather work with her than _____ (I/me).

   Using "I" would mean "Susan would rather work with her than I (would)," while using "me" would mean "Susan would rather work with her than (she would with) me."

C. Possessive

1. Possessive pronouns show ownership without the use of an apostrophe.

2. The possessive pronouns are "mine," "yours," "his," "hers," "its," "ours," and "theirs."

   Our papers have arrived but theirs have not.

D. Reflexive

1. Reflexive pronouns are used to refer back to the subject of a sentence.

2. The reflexive pronouns are "myself," "yourself," "himself," "herself," "itself," "ourselves," "yourselves," and "themselves."

   I worked myself to the bone.

V. GRAMMAR EXERCISE: PRONOUNS

A. Are the following sentences correct? Answer true if the sentence is correct and false if the sentence is incorrect.

1. ____ Her went to the store.

2. ____ It was me.

3. ____ We talked to him.

4. ____ It is myself.

5. ____ Talk to they before making a decision.

6. ____ Can you go with us?

7. ____ Sally and her have quit the team.

8. ____ They asked him and I to join.

9. ____ That call was for me, not he.

10. ____ You didn't tell us that they were here first.

11. ____ I wonder what he could have said to she.

12. ____ Between you and I, I think the deal is off.

13. ____ That invitation is for myself.

14. ____ Your sister and I are going to the party next week.

15. ____ She performed that play better than I.

16. ____ That is my new file.

17. ____ It is just myself staying late tonight.

18. ____ The training is only for you and she.

19. ____ Bob has more docketable hours this month than me.

20. ____ She talks to herself at lunch time.

VI. BEGINNER VOICE FILES

A. Beginner Voice File 1

Voice file: docs > CH11 > ch11beg1.mp3

Word template: docs > templates > letter.doc

Instructions: This is a letter. Use the letter template above or a template provided by your professor.

B. Beginner Voice File 2

Voice file: docs > CH11 > ch11beg2.mp3

Word template: docs > templates > letter.doc

Instructions: This is a letter. Use the letter template above or a template provided by your professor.

C. Beginner Voice File 3

Voice file: docs > CH11 > ch11beg3.mp3

Word template: docs > templates > voice.doc

Instructions: This is a voice message. Use the voice message template above or a template provided by your professor.

VII. INTERMEDIATE VOICE FILES

A. Intermediate Voice File 1

Voice file: docs > CH11 > ch11int1.mp3

Word template: docs > templates > memo.doc

Instructions: This is an interoffice memorandum. Use the interoffice memorandum template above or a template provided by your professor.

B. Intermediate Voice File 2

Voice file: docs > CH11 > ch11int2.mp3

Word template: docs > templates > voice.doc

Instructions: This is a voice message. Use the voice message template above or a template provided by your professor.

C. Intermediate Voice File 3

Voice file: docs > CH11 > ch11int3.mp3

Word template: docs > templates > letter.doc

Instructions: This is a letter. Use the letter template above or a template provided by your professor.

VIII. ADVANCED VOICE FILES

A. Advanced Voice File 1

Voice file: docs > CH11 > ch11adv1.mp3

Word template: docs > templates > letter.doc

Instructions: This is a letter. Use the letter template above or a template provided by your professor.

B. Advanced Voice File 2

Voice file: docs > CH11 > ch11adv2.mp3

Word template: docs > templates > letter.doc
                  docs > templates > account.doc

Instructions: This is a letter and statement of account. Use the letter and statement of account template above or a template provided by your professor.

C. Advanced Voice File 3

Voice file: docs > CH11 > ch11adv3.mp3

Word template: docs > templates > memo.doc

Instructions: This is an interoffice memorandum. Use the interoffice memorandum template above or a template provided by your professor.

CHAPTER 12

Small Claims

I. INTRODUCTION

This chapter will focus on the transcription tasks associated with **small claims court** files that are processed by law firms.

A. What Is a Small Claims Court Action?

A small claims court **action** is a court proceeding brought by one person, company, or corporation against another person, company, or corporation. The person making the claim - the **claimant** or **plaintiff** - is usually owed money or services. The claim must be made in one of the following jurisdictions:

1. The **jurisdiction** where the **incident** occurred

2. The jurisdiction where the defendant resides or carries on business

3. The jurisdiction of the court nearest to the defendant

Examples of small claims court cases are:

1. Broken verbal contracts

2. Broken written contracts

3. Car accident damages

4. Property damage

5. Landlord and tenant disputes

6. Bounced cheques

7. Unpaid wages

8. Unpaid personal debt

9. Unpaid services rendered

B. Lawyer or Paralegal?

Often individuals handle their own small claims court files without representation; however, due to the detailed nature of the process, many people choose to hire a legal professional to do the work for them. It is not necessary for a lawyer to prepare the documentation; a paralegal is permitted to speak before a **judge** in a small claims court action.

C. Amount Claimed

There is a maximum amount that can be claimed in a small claims court action. This amount varies by province and territory.

D. Time Limitations

There may be a **time limitation** on initiating a small claims court action. The time limitation will vary depending on the province or territory where the incident took place.

E. Steps to Making a Claim

1. The first step is a **plaintiff's claim** that is filed with the court on behalf of the claimant against the **defendant**, together with all supporting documents and the required filing fee.

2. The defendant may also make a **defendant's claim** against another person, company, or corporation. The defendant is also entitled to file a **defence**.

3. Each claim must be **served** on the opposing party.

4. An **affidavit of service** must be filed with the court proving that the claim was served properly.

5. If the defendant does not provide terms of **restitution** in the defence, the matter is **set down** for **trial**.

6. If the matter is not set down for trial and no other action occurs, the matter will be **dismissed**.

F. Mediation and Settlement

Note that **mediation** can occur at any time during the small claims court process up until the time that the judge issues a judgment in the case. A **settlement** between the parties is often less expensive than proceeding to trial, especially when a lawyer is involved.

G. Glossary Term Definitions

action	commencement of proceeding
affidavit of service	document detailing that a court document has been served on a party
claimant/plaintiff	person, company, or corporation commencing an action
defence	document filed in response to the commencement of an action
defendant	person, company, or corporation whom an action has been commenced against
defendant's claim	counterclaim or third-party claim filed by the defendant following the commencement of a claim
dismissed	an action is removed from the court system
incident	initiating event that resulted in the commencement of an action
judge	person presiding over the court who makes a decision as to which party is at fault in an action
jurisdiction	place where an event occurred, or where a party resides
mediation	attempt to reconcile the differences between two parties
plaintiff's claim	document filed to initiate an action
restitution	payment from one party to another in satisfaction of a claim
serve	to give a document to a party in a manner prescribed by the court
set down	set a date for a court trial
settlement	payment from one party to another in satisfaction of a claim
Small Claims Court	court allowing persons, companies, and corporations to make claims against other persons, companies, and corporations for payment of debts not exceeding amounts set by provincial and territorial legislation
time limitation	period of time after an incident has occurred that a claimant is entitled to file a claim
trial	court appearance where a judge decides the outcome of an action

II. TERMINOLOGY EXERCISE: SMALL CLAIMS

A. Fill in the blanks using the correct terminology found in the introduction:

John Johnston is one of our firm's clients. He has commenced a

_____ action against his neighbour for

damage to his property for a minimal amount. He has also filed an

_____, which is a legal document proving that the

claim was given to, or _____ on, the defendant. The neighbour

requested that they attend _____ with a neutral

party in an effort to resolve their issues without the need for a court

_____. The parties appeared to be in agreement over the

amount to be paid by the culpable party as _____.

This amount is to be paid by the _____. In the end,

the _____ offer, which was offered by the defendant in

an effort to settle the differences between the two parties, was refused by

our client. Our next step is to _____ the matter for trial

before the claim is _____ by the judge for missing the

deadline for filing of documentation. We are anxious to see what the

_____ will decide.

B. Fill in the blanks using the correct terminology found in the introduction:

Margaret Northrup has retained our firm to commence a small claims

court _____ against Paul Cyr with respect to a car accident.

The _____ occurred in the same town, or

_____, where the plaintiff and

_____ reside. Since we commenced the action, our

client's claim is known as the _____. The

defendant filed his defence, as well as a counterclaim, known as a

_____. The incident just occurred last month,

so we don't need to worry about the _____ as

we are still within the legal time frame to proceed. Our process server

delivered the documents and _____ the defendant with our

claim. Our next step will be to file an

_____ as proof that we have delivered the

documents to him.

III. CITATION EXERCISE

A. Rewrite each of the following by putting the units in the correct order with the correct punctuation:

1. *Small Claims Court Act*

   RSNS

   1989

   c 430

   _____

2. RSBC

   1996

   Small Claims Act

   c 430

   _____

3. 626/00

   O Reg

   Small Claims Court Jurisdiction

   _____

4. *Mayo v Veenstra*

   63 (volume)

   (2003)

   (3d)

   194 (page)

   (SC)

   OR

   _____

5. *Haines, Miller and Associates Inc v Foss*

   53 (page)

   153 (volume)

   NSR

   2d

   (1996)

   (SC)

   _____

6. 2005

    SKQB

    Saskatchewan Government Insurance v Valliere

    430

    270 (volume)

    Sask R

    47 (page)

    ---

7. c A.2

    Absconding Debtors Act

    1990

    RSO

    ---

8. *Brett Pontiac Buick GMC Ltd v American Home Assurance Company*

    2d

    116 (volume)

    NSR

    (1992)

    319 (page)

    (SC)

    ---

9. [1989]

    206 (page)

    Ontario (Attorney General) v Pembina Exploration Canada Ltd

    1 (volume)

    SCR

    ---

10. *Juker v Keith*

    2d

    99 (volume)

    BCLR

    (1994)

    262 (page)

    (SC)

B. **Rewrite each of the following citations by fixing all errors in format, spacing, and punctuation.**

1. Territorial Divisions for the Small Claims Court, RRO 1990 Reg206.

   _____

2. Bakaluk v. McGregor, 2003 SKQB 386 239 Sask R. 185.

   _____

3. Henson et al v Berkowits (2005) MBQB 32, 193 M.R. (2d) 170 (Q.B.).

   _____

4. Small Claims Court Act RSY 2002, c. 204

   _____

5. _Small Claims Court Taxation of Costs Regulations_, N.S. Reg. 37/2001.

   _____

6. Burchill v. Yukon Travel (1996) 28 BCLR 3d 95 (C.A.).

   _____

7. Small Claims Court - Fees and Allowances, O. Reg. 432/93.

   _____

8. _Sabine v. University of New Brunswick_ (1999) 210 N.B. R. (2nd) 86 (C.A.).

   _____

9. Wagg v. Canada, [2004] 1 FCR 206, 2003 FCA 303

   _____

10. Rocois Construction Inc. v. Québec Ready Mix Inc. [1990] 2 SCR 440

   _____

IV. HYPHENATION RULES: WORD DIVISION

A. Basic Word Division Rules

1. When using word-processing software, word division using hyphens does not apply, because the software keeps the words together.

2. Try to keep word groups on one line if they need to be read together, such as page 203, September 20xx, 10:30 a.m., 465 km, Mrs. Connolly and Paula Schein, M.D. Use a hard space (control + shift + space (PC); option + space (Mac)) to keep text together.

3. Dates may be broken between the day and year.

> . . . . is on January 31,
> 20xx.

4. Street addresses may be broken between the name of the street and type (e.g., Road, Avenue, Drive, etc.).

> . . . . .located at 111 Echo
> Drive.

5. Names of places (e.g., mailing addresses) may be broken between the city and the province or between the province and the postal code.

> . . . . .located in Ottawa,
> Ontario.

6. Names of persons may be broken between the given name (including middle name or initial if given) and surname.

> . . . . author is Lynn M.
> Berry.

> . . . . author is Barbara
> Asselin.

7. Names preceded by long titles may be broken between the title and the name

> . . . . Executive Vice President
> Susan Golding.

8. A numbered enumeration may be broken before (but not directly after) any number or letter.

> . . . . to discuss: 1. Minutes of previous meeting,
> 2. upcoming events, and 3. next meeting.

9. A sentence with a dash in it may be broken after the dash.

> . . . . they agreed to meet -
> if everyone is in the country - next Friday.

10. A sentence with ellipsis marks in it may be broken after the ellipsis marks.

> . . . . .litigation … real estate … corporate …
> intellectual property … we are a full service law firm.

V. HYPHENATION EXERCISE: WORD DIVISION

A. Are the following sentences true or false?

1. ____ Please come and visit me on Friday, October 31, 20xx. You can divide this sentence between *Friday* and *October* and between *31* and *20xx*.

2. ____ Her office is located at 1300 Carling Avenue in Ottawa. You can divide this sentence between *1300* and *Carling*.

3. ____ You can visit her in Kingston, Ontario. You can divide this sentence between *Kingston* and *Ontario*.

4. ____ This course ends in December 20xx. It is best not to divide between *December* and *20xx*.

5. ____ Please see me at 9:30 a.m. tomorrow. It is best to keep *a.m.* with *9:30*.

6. ____ Next semester - in February - we will be having a spring break. You can divide this sentence after both dashes.

7. ____ Mrs. Janice O'Reilly was here as a guest speaker. You can divide this sentence after *Janice*.

8. ____ Please do the following: (1) undertake your proofreading homework, (2) contact your mentor, and (3) read the Minutes from Program Council. You can divide this sentence after *(1)*, *(2)* or *(3)*.

9. ____ Document production ... keyboarding ... computer studies ... are several areas of your program. You can divide this sentence after any of the ellipsis marks.

10. ____ Vice-President Judy Gilliland is sometimes involved with the School of Business. You could divide this sentence after *President*.

11. ____ Please arrange a meeting in the second floor boardroom at 11 a.m. and invite Mr. Tillman. You could divide this sentence after *11*.

12. ____ An analysis of the sales data indicates that we broke even by the end of the fiscal year January 31, 20xx. You could divide this sentence after *31*.

13. ____ The letter should be addressed to the recipient, Mr. Pierre Denault, who resides at 1421 Bankfield Road, Ottawa. You could divide this sentence after *Denault* or after *Bankfield*.

14. ____ In the event that the accounting office requires a statement, it can be submitted to Kevin Nelson, the new city councillor. You could divide this sentence after *statement* or after *Nelson*.

15. ____ The alarm system also has several stationary hold-up buttons permanently mounted in the house. Your software will automatically divide this sentence as necessary.

16. ___ In the event that you have not received the cheque and/or notification of cancellation, please contact me, and I will make sure the matter is speedily resolved. You can divide this sentence after the /.

17. ___ The weekly meeting has been scheduled for the Mortgage Management Department staff at 10 a.m. in the main staff room. It doesn't matter where this sentence is divided.

18. ___ I find the terms of the agreement to be acceptable; however, you may want to have Lester R. Brown review them, too. You can divide this sentence after *acceptable*.

19. ___ I've reviewed each of the hotels and determined that only the Best Western can accommodate our group. This sentence can be divided anywhere.

20. ___ In addition, there is a lot of interest for word processing and spreadsheets, as indicated on page 234 of the report. This sentence can be divided after *page*.

VI. BEGINNER VOICE FILES

A. Beginner Voice File 1

Voice file: docs > CH12 > ch12beg1.mp3

Word template: docs > templates > letter.doc

Instructions: This is a letter. Use the letter template above or a template provided by your professor.

B. Beginner Voice File 2

Voice file: docs > CH12 > ch12beg2.mp3

Word template: docs > templates > letter.doc

Instructions: This is a letter. Use the letter template above or a template provided by your professor.

C. Beginner Voice File 3

Voice file: docs > CH12 > ch12beg3.mp3

Word template: docs > templates > voice.doc

Instructions: This is a voice message. Use the voice message template above or a template provided by your professor.

VII. INTERMEDIATE VOICE FILES

A. Intermediate Voice File 1

Voice file: docs > CH12 > ch12int1.mp3

Word template: docs > templates > memo.doc

Instructions: This is an interoffice memorandum. Use the interoffice memorandum template above or a template provided by your professor.

B. Intermediate Voice File 2

Voice file: docs > CH12 > ch12int2.mp3

Word template: docs > templates > voice.doc

Instructions: This is a voice message. Use the voice message template above or a template provided by your professor.

C. Intermediate Voice File 3

Voice file: docs > CH12 > ch12int3.mp3

Word template: docs > templates > letter.doc

Instructions: This is a letter. Use the letter template above or a template provided by your professor.

VIII. ADVANCED VOICE FILES

A. Advanced Voice File 1

Voice file: docs > CH12 > ch12adv1.mp3

Word template: docs > templates > letter.doc

Instructions: This is a letter. Use the letter template above or a template provided by your professor.

B. Advanced Voice File 2

Voice file: docs > CH12 > ch12adv2.mp3

Word template: docs > templates > letter.doc

docs > templates > account.doc

Instructions: This is a letter and statement of account. Use the letter and statement of account template above or a template provided by your professor.

C. Advanced Voice File 3

Voice file: docs > CH12 > ch12adv3.mp3

Word template: docs > templates > memo.doc

Instructions: This is an interoffice memorandum. Use the interoffice memorandum template above or a template provided by your professor.

Glossary

abandonment application is not registered

access when the non-custodial parent spends time with the child of the marriage

accused person charged with a criminal offence

acquittal ruling that the accused is not guilty

action commencement of proceeding

adjournment postponement of a trial until a later date

adultery ground for divorce when one spouse has had an extra-marital affair

advertised application is made public knowledge

advertisement application is advertised in journal

affidavit of service document detailing that a court document has been served on a party

agent person acting on behalf of someone, such as the owner of a property; individual working for an intellectual property company who assists in getting application approved through CIPO

agreement of purchase and sale agreement between purchaser and vendor setting out terms under which the purchaser will become the owner of the property

allowance if there is no opposition to application, application is approved and is ready for registration

answer document that is filed in response to the application for divorce

application court document and process of applying for probate and appointment of estate trustee; initial submission to CIPO in the process of receiving intellectual property right

application for divorce document that is filed to initiate divorce proceedings

approval application is approved by CIPO

arrest detainment of an individual accused of having committed a crime for probable cause

articles of incorporation form required by government that includes details of incorporated company

at the suit (ats) being litigated against (sued)

attorney/grantee/donee person who is given authority over assets or personal care by the grantor

bail surety (money or property) pledged or deposited with the court for the release of the accused with a guarantee that the accused will appear in court on the date assigned

bail hearing hearing at which a judge determines whether an accused can be released

bench warrant order of a judge authorizing the police to locate and arrest an accused for failing to appear in court

beneficiaries people named in a will to receive property as a result of the will

bequest property gifted through a will or succession

bounce of a cheque, to be returned by a bank when there are insufficient funds in the payor's bank account to cover the payment

bylaws rules adopted by a company defining its internal governance

capital money invested by a shareholder into a company

case conference procedural step in divorce process dealing with issues such as scheduling and appointing a children's lawyer

chattels items that will remain in the property when the purchaser becomes the owner

child support amount paid from one spouse to the other spouse to help pay for the expenses of the children of the marriage

CIPO Canadian Intellectual Property Office, responsible for administering and processing intellectual property

civil litigation legal dispute between parties

claimant/plaintiff person, company, or corporation commencing an action

class action suit a group of people who collectively bring a claim against a defendant

closing date the date on which the purchaser will become the owner of the property

codicil legal document making minor changes to a will

conditions items in the agreement of purchase and sale for the benefit of either the vendor or the purchaser, which must be met in order for the agreement to become a firm and binding contract

condominium unit where the owner owns the unit only and is part owner in the exterior of the building and the common elements

conflict of interest occurs when opposing parties are represented by the same law firm

consent document signed by a party to a transaction acknowledging a potential conflict of interest as a result of the fact that the lawyer is acting for both sides

continuing power of attorney for property tends to financial matters and is to be used when grantor is rendered unable to act on behalf of himself or herself

conviction ruling that an accused is guilty

copyright protection of expression and exclusive right to an author's original work

corporate minute book book that contains all pertinent documents of a corporation

corporate seal device used to emboss the impression of a company name onto a document

corporation company that has been incorporated under either provincial or federal laws

court or tribunal action proceeding between two parties where a presiding body decides a disputed action

Crown attorney Crown lawyer who represents the victim

cruelty ground for divorce when one spouse was victimized by the other

custodial parent parent with sole custody of the children of the marriage

damages compensation for injury or other losses

declaration sworn statement of entitlement to intellectual property, which is part of application

default fail to make payments previously agreed to

defence document filed in response to the commencement of an action

defence attorney lawyer who represents the accused

defendant party to whom a claim is made against; person, company, or corporation whom an action has been commenced against

defendant's claim counterclaim or third-party claim filed by the defendant following the commencement of a claim

demand letter legal letter sent to opposing party requesting compensation in advance of litigation

Department of Justice department of the federal government dealing with procedures of divorce in Canada

deposit amount of money paid by the purchaser to the vendor to show "good faith" that they will complete the transaction

direction re: title document signed by purchaser detailing how the purchaser wishes to take title to the property such as joint tenancy or tenants in common

directors individuals appointed within a corporation to direct the affairs of the company

disclosure process required before a trial in which the police provide the defence attorney with a summary of the charges and the evidence against the accused

discovery procedural step in divorce process where parties exchange financial and other information; process whereby evidence and documents to be used at trial are disclosed and reviewed

dismiss plaintiff puts aside an action

dismissed an action is removed from the court system

divorce dissolution of marriage

divorce certificate document certifying that parties are divorced

duplex a house divided into two apartments

emboss create an impression onto a document using a seal

estate assets on death (real and personal property)

estate trustee court-appointed person authorized to distribute estate in Ontario

evidence facts, which may or may not be in dispute, pertaining to a case

examination application is reviewed in detail

examiner CIPO employee who reviews application and writes a report based on the findings of the examination

execute sign a document

executor/executrix person named in a will to administer and distribute the estate; court-appointed person authorized to distribute an estate

expert witness witness hired for his or her specific knowledge, skill, or experience in a particular field

Express Scribe free, downloadable software used to listen to voice files while transcribing them in a separate word-processing software

federal child support guidelines means of calculating child support based on income of parties and number of children of the marriage

filing application is made to CIPO

financial statement document itemizing the income and expenses of an individual

first month's rent first monthly rental payment

fixtures items that are fixed to the property

flat fee/block fee accounts all-inclusive set fees for legal services performed

floater an administrative staff member who "floats" around the firm in different administrative positions, usually to fill in for staff that are sick or on vacation; also works on overflow duties when a particular staff member has more work than can be done by one person

freehold a dwelling that is owned solely by the individual who purchases a property

grantor/donor person granting authority to attorney to act on his or her behalf in regard to assets or personal care

guarantor an individual or company that guarantees mortgage payments to the mortgagee in the event that the mortgagor defaults on mortgage payments

guardian person named in a will to have the authority to care for the testator's minor children

guilty plea in which an accused admits to the charges

hearsay indirect knowledge of an event, also called third-party knowledge

hot keys keystrokes or keystroke combinations that cause specific reactions for a specific software

incarceration confinement of a person convicted of an offence to a correctional facility to serve a sentence

incident initiating event that resulted in the commencement of an action

incorporate prepare necessary documentation in order to register a company

indictable offence serious offence that may be punishable by fines over $5,000 and sentences greater than six months

industrial design protection of the original shape, pattern, or ornamentation of an article that is mass-produced

infringement owner's Intellectual property rights are violated

inquiry letters letters sent by the law firm representing a purchaser to various utility and municipal departments requesting information on the status of the account of the current property owner

integrated circuit topographies protected three-dimensional configurations of the electronic circuits used in microchips and semiconductor chips

intellectual property exclusive rights over creations of the mind

intestate condition arising when someone dies without a valid will

judge person presiding over the court who makes a decision as to which party is at fault in an action

judgment decision made by judge at trial

judicial pre-trial conferences conferences in which defence and Crown attorneys attempt to resolve a matter to avoid going to trial

jurisdiction place where an event occurred, or where a party resides

jury Canadian citizens brought together for trial to reach a verdict on an action

keyboard shortcuts see "hot keys" above

landlord owner of a rental property

last month's rent security deposit in the amount of one month's rent that will be applied toward the tenant's final month of residence in a rental property

last will and testament (will) legal document outlining one's wishes on death in terms of distribution of estate property

lease document providing details of agreement between landlord and tenant

legislation government-regulated rules that set out procedures in certain areas of law

limitation periods legally mandated time frames by which actions must be commenced

liquidated damages those damages determined on the face of the documents between the parties or by established standards

mediation attempt to reconcile the differences between two parties

memorandum sets out rules for the conduct of an incorporated company

mentally incompetent unable to understand the consequences of one's decisions

minor child under the age of 18

minutes record of meeting of members of an incorporated company

month-to-month lease agreement between landlord and tenant regarding a rental property where parties are not bound for a one-year term

mortgage document (also known as a "charge") registered against a property to secure the loan of monies from a financial institution to a property owner

mortgagee financial institution that lends money to property owners and secures the loan by registration of a mortgage

mortgagor property owner who borrows money from a financial institution

motion court procedure allowing parties in an action to apply for a ruling on a particular issue before the final judgment is reached

multi-unit dwelling three or more dwelling units in one building where the units are on multiple levels of the building

negligence causing harm to another through carelessness; the most common form of a tort

new home construction new home constructed by a builder

non-disclosure agreement binding document signed between two parties whereby ideas discussed will be kept confidential

notarial certificate legal document authenticating that the attached document is an exact duplicate of the original

notice provision of information as required by law to make the recipient aware of a fact or thing

notice of directors document detailing the directors of an incorporated company

notice of offices document detailing a company's registered office and records office

notice of rent increase document sent from landlord to tenant advising that the fees for residing in the rental property will be increasing

notice to vacate the premises document sent from landlord to tenant providing notice that the tenant must vacate the premises and providing details regarding the reasons why and the time by which the tenant must vacate

NUANS search search for availability of a company name

numbered company incorporated company with no specific name; rather, it is assigned the next number of incorporated companies, e.g., 101568 Canada Inc., Ltd., Limited, or Incorporated

offer to settle an invitation by a party to settle an action

officers individuals within a corporation that hold a specific office, such as president or secretary

opposition occurs when a claim is made against application

partnership two or more individuals that start a business detailed through a partnership agreement instead of a corporation

patent protected invention that is new, useful, and unique in terms of its mechanism or operation

payment direction direction signed by the vendor(s) in a transaction detailing how the balance due on closing is to be paid

per stirpes clause in a will that entitles heirs of a beneficiary to receive property in the event of a beneficiary's death

personal liability legal and financial responsibility of an individual with respect to the debts and obligations of a business

personal property chattels or all property other than real estate, including bank accounts, investments, and valuable items

plagiarism claiming someone else's work a your own without permission of the author

plaintiff the party bringing an action against another

plaintiff's claim document filed to initiate an action

plant breeders' rights protected rights to new varieties of certain plant species

plea an answer of "guilty" or "not guilty" in response to a charge

pleadings court documents outlining claims by both parties

post-dated cheques cheques given from tenant to landlord that are dated in the future and will cover upcoming rental payments

power of attorney for personal care tends to health-care needs and is to be used when grantor is rendered unable to act on behalf of himself or herself

powers of attorney legal devices giving authority to others to act on one's behalf

pre-trial conference process in which an attempt is made to resolve matter before trial

prepaid rent rental payments that have been paid in advance of their due dates

pro bono provision of legal services free of charge

probate court process of validating last will and testament and appointing an estate trustee

process server individual who delivers court documents to parties named on documents

property land that may or may not include one or more dwelling units that is the subject of a purchase, sale, or mortgage transaction

purchase the act of an individual or a company buying a property from another individual or company

purchaser person or company buying a property from another person or company

real property real estate

register document within a corporate minute book containing all entries pertaining to a certain aspect of the corporation

registered application receives approval by CIPO

registered business name name under which a company will operate its business

registration final approval of application and application is registered

rent amount paid from tenant to landlord in exchange for the right to occupy the rental property

rental items items that the vendor currently rents and that the purchaser will continue to rent following closing

rental period amount of time that a tenant is permitted to occupy a rental property

rental property property that is the subject of a lease

reply document filed with the court to dispute claims in the answer previously filed by the other party

requisition date the date by which the purchaser's lawyer must have reviewed the title search and submitted the requisition letter to the vendor's lawyer

requisition letter correspondence sent from the purchaser's lawyer to the vendor's lawyer detailing any problems uncovered by the title search, building location survey, inquiry letters, or agreement of purchase and sale that need to be corrected prior to closing

resale home a home that was owned by several companies or individuals prior to being sold to a purchaser

resolutions details of actions agreed to by either the directors or the shareholders of a corporation

restitution court-ordered payment of compensation for damage caused or gain made as a result of criminal activity by an individual convicted of an offence to the victim; payment from one party to another in satisfaction of a claim

retain to hire a law firm for representation

retainer official hiring of a law firm for representation. Also known as the amount of money paid in trust to the firm in advance

revoke cancel the authority

row house three or more dwelling units side by side in one building

royalties percentage of revenue paid to intellectual property owners for sale or use of their work

rules and regulations terms outlining the obligations of the parties in an agreement

sale the transfer of ownership of a home or property from one person or company to another person or company in exchange for financial compensation

sale price amount of money to be paid by the purchaser to the vendor for the purchase of a property

searches determining if intellectual property already exists

securities certificate showing ownership

semi-detached home two dwelling units side by side in one building

separation two parties of a marriage living separate and apart

separation agreement document detailing the terms on which the parties of a marriage will live separate and apart

serve to give a document to a party in a manner prescribed by the court

service delivery of legal documents to parties involved

set down set a date for a court trial

settlement payment from one party to another in satisfaction of a claim

settlement conference procedural step in divorce process that attempts to resolve the outstanding issues in a divorce, thereby eliminating the need to proceed to trial

share certificate document detailing the number of shares owned by an individual or a company within a corporation

shared custody children of the marriage spend at least 40 percent of the time with each parent

shareholder person or company that owns shares in a corporation

shares division of equity in a corporation

single family home single home on a piece of land

Small Claims Court court allowing persons, companies, and corporations to make claims against other persons, companies, and corporations for payment of debts not exceeding amounts set by provincial and territorial legislation

sole custody children of the marriage spend the majority of the time with one parent, the custodial parent

split custody one or more children of the marriage spend the majority of the time with one parent, and one or more children of the marriage spend the majority of the time with the other parent

spousal support advisory guidelines means of calculating spousal support based on the income and expenses of the parties

spousal support spouse with the higher income pays an amount to the spouse with the lower income, in an effort to lessen the effects of divorce

start-up costs amount of money required to set up a corporation

statement of adjustments document setting out the financial details of the property resulting in a balance due on closing

statement of claim originating document sent by the plaintiff outlining the relevant law and facts and the restitution sought

statement of defence responding document to statement of claim outlining defendant's position

statutory declarations documents sworn or declared by either purchasers or vendors that contain true statements necessary to complete a real estate transaction

succession laws set of laws that use spousal relationships or bloodlines to determine heirs and the distribution of assets in cases where an individual dies intestate

summary conviction offence less serious offence usually punishable by fine of up to $5,000 and/or sentence of up to six months

summons legal document issued by a court ordering an individual to appear before the court and outlining the reasons for the appearance

tenant person entitled to live at a rental property in exchange for payment of rent to the landlord

testate condition arising when one dies with a valid will in place

testator/testatrix person making a will

testimony formal statements made by witnesses under oath before a court

time limitation period of time after an incident has occurred that a claimant is entitled to file a claim

title insurance policy purchased by purchasers and mortgagees protecting them from certain unknown problems affecting a property

title insurance direction document signed by purchaser directing lawyer to purchase a title insurance policy

title of proceeding header on court documents that outlines the parties involved

title search compilation of documents prepared by a title searcher detailing all documents affecting a certain property

title searcher individual who searches property for ownership and other claims filed against the property

tort a wrong or an injury suffered by a person for which another person can be held liable

trade name business name

trade-mark protected distinctive identity of a product, such as its words, symbols, logo, pictures, and designs

transfer document that transfers ownership from one party to another

trial hearing of a matter before a judge or before a judge and jury; last step in a divorce action, wherein a judge decides the outstanding issues based on evidence received from the parties and other witnesses

trustee person given the authority to administer assets on behalf of a third party; for example, minor children

undertaking document signed by a party promising to complete a task within a certain time frame

unliquidated damages damages that are undetermined and need to be assessed by the court

UPOV International Union for the Protection of New Varieties of Plants, responsible for plant breeders' rights

utilities services to a property provided by a company supplying water, gas, and hydro

vacant land land where no dwelling unit exists

vendor person or company selling a property to another person or company

verdict ruling by a judge or a judge and jury regarding disputed issues in a trial

versus (v.) litigating against (suing)

victim in a criminal case, the person wronged

waiver legal document releasing the estate trustee of further obligations to the estate

warrant document issued by a judge or other official authorizing the police to make an arrest or perform other acts related to the administration of justice

witness person who has first-hand knowledge of an alleged crime

witnesses people over the age of 18 who validate that the document was properly executed